Also from Brassey's:

Brassey's Book of Camouflage
Brassey's Book of Uniforms

Brassey's History of Uniforms

American Civil War: Confederate Army
American Civil War: Union Army
Napoleonic Wars: Wellington's Army
Napoleonic Wars: Napoleon's Army
Mexican-American War 1846-48
English Civil War
Roman Army: Wars of the Empire
Barbarian Warriors: Saxons, Vikings, Normans
Spanish-American War 1898
World War One: British Army
World War One: German Army
British Army: Zulu War to Boer War

Brassey's *History of Uniforms*

Spanish-American War 1898

By Ron Field

Colour plates by Richard Hook

Series editor Tim Newark

Brassey's London • Washington

To Judy Wray and Shara Spragg.

First English Edition 1998

UK editorial offices: Brassey's Ltd, 33 John Street, London
WC1N 2AT
UK Orders: Marston Book Services, PO Box 269, Abingdon,
OX14 4SD

North American Orders: Brassey's Inc,
PO Box 960, Herndon, VA 22070, USA

Ron Field has asserted his moral right to be identified as the
author of this work.

Library of Congress Cataloging in Publication Data available
British Library Cataloguing in Publication Data
A catalogue record for this book is available from the British
Library

ISBN 1 85753 272 4 Hardcover

Typeset by Hedgehog, Upton-upon-Severn, Worcestershire.

Printed and bound in Singapore
under the supervision of M.R.M. Graphics Ltd,
Winslow, Buckinghamshire.

Contents

Introduction

The Spanish-American War of 1898, and the consequent Philippine Insurrection which lasted until 1902, represent a remarkable period of transition in American military history. The conflict involved the United States Army in its first overseas campaigns, and saw a revolutionary change in uniforms and weapons. It was also a turning point in the colonial history of Spain. Although Spanish riflemen fought heroically at El Caney and San Juan Heights, their capitulation in Cuba during August of 1898 resulted in the ultimate loss of all Spanish colonies in the Caribbean and the Pacific.

The outbreak of hostilities in April 1898 found the American land forces wearing blue wool uniforms which were entirely unsuitable for warfare in the subtropics. By July 1902, when the last Filipino freedom fighters finally surrendered, the American army had been transformed into a khaki-clad modern force. In comparison, the loose-fitting *rayadillo*, or

Several of these unidentified U.S. Volunteers wear the VIII Corps badge, which probably indicates they were photographed in the Philippines. They wear the typical dark blue overshirt, blue woven cartridge belt fastened by an 'H'-shaped plate, and M1889 drab felt campaign hat. The man standing in the left foreground has shaped his hat into the unofficial, but fashionable, 'Montana' peak. They are armed with 'Trapdoor' Springfield rifles. Ron Da Silva Collection.

The U.S.S. *Maine* is blown up in Havana Harbour, 15 February 1898. Peter Newark's Military Pictures.

fine-striped, cotton uniforms worn by the Spanish Colonial Army for decades were more appropriate to conditions in both Cuba and the Philippines.

Learning from bitter battle experience in Cuba, where the black powder cartridge gave away the position of American riflemen to Spanish forces armed with smokeless Mauser rifles, the U.S. Ordnance Department wisely adopted the first 'smokeless powder' firearms to be used by the Army. The period also saw the first widespread use by the U.S. Army of magazine longarms, namely the Krag-Jörgensen rifle and carbine, which were chosen above other arms after extensive trials conducted during the early 1890s. Meanwhile, Dr. Richard Gatling, Civil War inventor of a machine gun capable of firing 600 rounds per minute, saw his deadly weapon cover the advance of the 'thin blue line' of American soldiers as they launched their final assault on San Juan Ridge, before his death in 1903. The use of compressed air to hurl rocks dates back to the time of Alexander the Great – but it took the combination of Captain Edmund Zalinski, a Polish-born American who became a prolific inventor, the U.S. Navy gunboat *Vesuvius*, and

the Spanish-American War, to put it all into practice in the form of the short-lived pneumatic dynamite gun! Less successful was the service of the Balloon Detachment of the 5th U.S. Army Corps in Cuba. Led by Major Joseph E. Maxfield, U.S. Volunteer Signals, this unit provided useful overhead views of the Spanish positions from a hot-air balloon which ascended near General William R. Shafter's headquarters, about one and a half miles from the battle lines. But when unwisely moved forward along the trail leading to the front, the silver monster promptly drew Spanish fire, and consequently on the U.S. troops moving beneath it!

The frenzied charges of the bolo-wielding, Christian-hating *Moro*, or Mohammedan, population of the island of Mindanao in the Philippines, struck terror into the hearts of many a young American Volunteer as the U.S. continued to consolidate its occupation of the Philippines at the turn of the century. As Filipino insurgents went underground, the U.S. Army found itself fighting against a guerrilla force reminiscent of that met in the jungles of Vietnam 70 years later. At the end of this tumultuous period, the United States of America emerged as a new world power and would go on to play a leading role in the political and military history of the 20th

A rare image of Spanish Riflemen in Cuba wearing *rayadillo* uniforms and *gorro de cuartel*, or barracks caps, receiving weapons training with Model 1871 single shot Remington rifles. Note the 'buglehorn' collar insignia, and medals proudly worn by the man fourth from the right. The photographer's backmark reads 'A. Desquiron, Sn Geronimo baja 8, Stgo. de Cuba.' Museo del Ejército, Madrid.

century.

The seeds of the conflict which took the United States along this path were planted in the Spanish colony of Cuba at the beginning of the 19th century. Although permitted considerable commercial freedom in return for loyalty to Ferdinand VII in 1808, the 'Ever Faithful Isle' continued to be ruled from Madrid by a repressive political regime. Several attempts at rebellion between 1820 and 1830, fomented by secret societies such as the 'Soles de Bolivar' and the 'Black Eagle', were quickly suppressed, and led to a tightening of the despotic control of the captains general of Cuba. A further conspiracy against Spanish rule in 1844 led to the execution of the Cuban poet Placido.

Meanwhile, American designs on Cuba were growing. In 1820, John C. Calhoun of South Carolina had stressed Cuba's importance as 'not only the first commercial and military position in the world', but as 'the keystone to our Union. No American statesman ought ever to draw his eye from it.'[1] In the wake of success following the war with Mexico, President James K. Polk announced in 1848: 'I am decidedly in favour of purchasing Cuba & making it one of the States of [the] Union.'[2] This idea was of particular appeal to southerners such as Senator Jefferson Davis of Mississippi who declared that 'Cuba must be ours' in order to 'increase the slaveholding constituencies'.[3] An annexationist pamphlet of the day described the island as: 'The Pearl of the West Indies', who 'with her thirteen to fifteen representatives in Congress would be a powerful auxiliary to the South'.[4] President Polk attempted to buy Cuba for $100 million, but was informed by the Spanish foreign minister that Spain would 'prefer seeing it sunk in the ocean'.[5] Official American designs on Cuba were thwarted in 1848 by the election to the presidency of Mexican War hero Zachary Taylor, whose Whig Party policies were anti-expansionist.

The annexationists next placed their hopes in Narciso López, a Venezuelan soldier of fortune who had fled to New York in 1848 after a failed attempt to organise a revolt against Spanish rule among the Cuban planters. Recruiting a small army of about 350

A Moro group. The two men in the middle row seated second and third from the left are clearly dignatories, and possibly sultans. Rank may be indicated by the batons they both hold, whilst the man in the centre wears a broad sash. Note the foot officer's sword attached to the belt of the man to his left. The braid on the war shirts of at least four of the others may suggest evidence of a uniform. Museo del Ejército, Madrid.

Cuban exiles and Mexican War veterans, or 'filibusters' (from the Spanish *filibustero*, meaning freebooter or pirate), he initially asked Jefferson Davis, who later in 1861 became the first and only president of the Confederate States of America, to lead the planned invasion to liberate Cuba. Davis refused but recommended his friend Robert E. Lee, who also politely declined the offer. Taking command himself during September, 1849, López planned a two-prong assault on Cuba – one expedition setting sail from New York and another from tiny Round Island off Mississippi's Gulf coast. Successfully nipping the venture in the bud, U.S. Government agents seized four ships, weapons, and ammunition.

Undaunted, López planned a second expedition which successfully set off from New Orleans on board the steamer *Creole* in May 1850. Largely financed, armed, and supplied by John Quitman, governor of Mississippi, about 500 filbusters dressed in red shirts and oil-skin caps, landed at Cardenas, on the north coast of Cuba, on the 19th of that month.[6] López's soldiers took possession of the town and burned the governor's mansion, but were disappointed when the local Cuban population failed to answer their plea for reinforcements. Subsequently surrounded by Spanish troops which included 'the corps of mounted artillery

and lancers', López's filibusters were forced to withdraw to their vessel which barely outraced the Spanish war steamer *Pizarro* back to Key West.[7] Indicted for violation of the Neutrality Act of 1818 and the 1797 friendship pact between Spain and the United States, López, Quitman and several other Southerners were called to stand trial in New Orleans, but after three trials of one defendent ended in hung juries, the federal government dropped the remaining indictments.

Thus vindicated, the filibusters were free to organise another expedition against Cuba in 1851. On 3 August, the steamer *Pampero* slipped out of New Orleans with López's 'army' of 400 composed of six companies of infantry, three companies of artillery, one company of Cuban patriots, and two small detachments of Hungarians and Germans. Landing near Bahia Honda on the western end of the island, they found Spanish troops ready and waiting. In the ensuing battles at Las Pozas and Carambola, 200 filibusters were killed and the rest, including López, were captured.[8] Spanish authorities ordered López to be garroted in front of a large crowd in Havana, whilst the remainder of his 'army' was either shot by firing squad or shipped to Spain to work in the quicksilver mines. When news reached New Orleans, rioting mobs destroyed the Spanish consulate and sacked stores owned by Spaniards. The *New Orleans Courier* demanded: 'Blood for Blood! Our brethren must be avenged! Cuba must be seized!'[9]

From 1851 to 1868 the smouldering fires of revolt among Cubans found little chance of breaking into flames, despite the growth in the United States of the 'Order of the Lone Star', a clandestine organisation of 'several thousand' men sworn to avenge López, and free Cuba.[10] The revolution of September 1868, which drove Queen Isabella II from Spain, furnished an occasion which the Cuban freedom fighters were not slow to take advantage of. On 10 October, the independence of Cuba was proclaimed by Carlos de Céspedes, who soon had a force of 15,000 men marching under his orders. During April, 1869, a

A contemporary map of Cuba. From Murat Halstead, 'Full Official History of the War with Spain' (1899).

congress assembled at Guáymaro framed a constitution, and elected Céspedes as president. The ensuing conflict with Spain, known as the Ten Years' War, lasted until 1878. For the first two years of guerilla warfare, the Cuban forces seemed to have the upper hand, despite their inferior arms and equipment. Of more than 150,000 Spanish troops committed to this war, some 80,000 are believed to have found their graves in Cuba. However, dissension in their own ranks eventually weakened the Cuban cause and resulted in the capitulation at El Zanjon in 1878, by which Spain vainly agreed to reform her rule of the island and to allow Cuban representation at the Cortes at Madrid.

Disillusioned by broken promises, the Cubans turned again to revolution in 1895. The resulting brutal treatment of Cuban insurgents by the Spanish Army received much publicity in the U.S., chiefly through reports published in the New York press. Concern also grew over the extensive damage to property caused by the war. Considerable American investments were affected, and all U.S. trade with Cuba was halted. Popular demand for intervention on behalf of Cuban independence gained wide support in Congress, but President William McKinley, like his predecessor, President Grover Cleveland, firmly opposed U.S. action. In 1897 the Spanish Prime

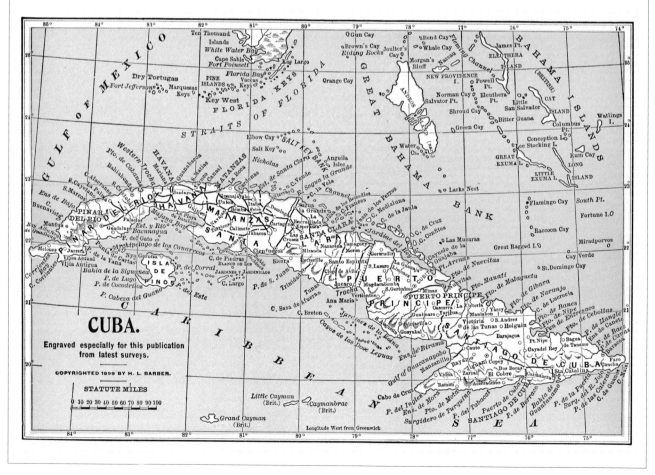

Minister, Práxedes Mateo Sagasta, attempted to settle the conflict by granting partial autonomy to Cuba. He also promised to abolish the system of prison camps which had caused such widespread outrage on the island. The freedom fighters remained unappeased, however, and continued to fight for complete independence.

A further series of incidents in 1897 finally brought about U.S. intervention. During December of that year the U.S. battleship *Maine* was despatched to the port of Havana to protect American citizens and property. On the night of 15 February 1898, this vessel was sunk by a huge explosion, with the loss of 266 lives. Although evidence pointed to sabotage, responsibility for the disaster was never determined.

During the following month, Senator Redfield Proctor of Vermont made a stirring speech in the Senate, which described inhumane conditions observed in Cuba. On 19 April 1898, the U.S. Congress authorised President McKinley to use the army and navy of the United States to force Spain to renounce its sovereignty over Cuba. The next day, McKinley approved a congressional resolution calling for the immediate Spanish withdrawal from Cuba. On 24 April 1898, Spain declared war on the United States, and the following day Congress finally

Lieutenant John H. Parker, 13th U.S. Infantry, and his Gatling Gun Detachment below San Juan Hill on 1 July 1898. Painting by Charles McBarron. Peter Newark's Military Pictures.

announced that hostilities had officially begun on 21 April. Thus, for the first time for over half a century, the United States was at war with a foreign country. What followed according to U.S. Secretary of State John Hay was 'a splendid little war' which only lasted ten weeks in Cuba and Puerto Rico, but subsequently developed into the Philippines Insurrection which dragged on until 4 July 1902.

'A Splendid Little War'

The first action of the Spanish-American War took place in the Far East and the Pacific. As part of contingency plans for a possible war with Spain, an attack on Manila in the Philippines had long been contemplated as a diversion from the main American assault on Cuba in the Caribbean. Ten days after the sinking of the *Maine*, Commodore George Dewey, Commander-in-Chief of the U.S. Naval Force, Asiatic Station, was ordered to proceed with his squadron to the British colony of Hong Kong and there to prepare for action in the Philippines. Two months later, on 24 April 1898, he finally received instructions to 'commence operations against the Spanish squadron'.[11]

At dawn on 1 May, Dewey found an ill-prepared Spanish Asiatic Squadron anchored in Manila Bay. Ordering his six cruisers to steam in an open elliptical pattern, he then informed the captain of his flagship *Olympia*: 'You may fire when ready, Gridley.' Within six hours, ten Spanish vessels, including the flagship *Reina Christina*, and the cruisers *Isla de Cuba* and *Castilla*, had been destroyed, with the loss of 381 Spaniards killed and wounded.[12]

Having accepted the surrender of Spanish Admiral Montijo, resulting in the capture of the arsenal and naval base at Cavite, Dewey lacked sufficient land forces to exploit his success any further, and consequently entered into an uneasy alliance with Emilio Aguinaldo, the leader of the Philippines independence movement. Meanwhile, on 4 May, President McKinley ordered U.S. troops to San Francisco and then to the Philippines to occupy Manila.

In the Atlantic, the Spanish Squadron under Admiral Pascual de Cervera, consisting of three armoured cruisers, one battleship, and three torpedo gunboats, gathered at the Portuguese Cape Verde Islands. Its presence where it could be launched westward at any time caused much alarm in Washington, D.C., and fear that Cervera might attempt to intercept the U.S. battleship *Oregon* which was making haste around South America from San Francisco to reinforce the American Atlantic fleet. Sailing from the Cape Verde Islands on 29 April, Cervera evaded detection and slipped into the harbour of Santiago de Cuba early on 19 May for much needed repairs, provisions, and coal.

Learning of Cervera's whereabouts via a confidential agent in the Havana telegraph office, the U.S. Atlantic fleet under Rear Admiral William T. Sampson steamed at full speed into the Caribbean and arrived off Santiago on 28 May. This effectively bottled him up, and prevented Cervera from threatening America's shores or bringing succour to Spain's other Caribbean possessions. However, the U.S. Navy could not now reach the Spanish ships which were protected by coastal batteries and mines, and the unlikely event of the U.S. Army being called upon to capture a foreign fleet became a reality!

On 30 May 1898, Major General William R. Shafter, U.S.V., commanding the U.S. Fifth Army Corps gathered at Tampa, Florida, received orders to proceed under naval escort to the 'vicinity of Santiago de Cuba' to seize 'the high ground and bluffs, overlooking the harbor ... and with the aid of the navy capture or destroy the Spanish fleet...'[13] A veteran of the Civil War, Shafter had acquired the nick-name 'Pecos Bill' while commanding the black 24th Infantry Regiment in West Texas during the 1870s. Promoted to Brigadier General in 1897, he was appointed to the command of the Department of the Pacific, and held this post when the war with Spain began.

Modelled on the old Fifth Corps of the Civil War Army of the Potomac, Shafter's command contained a high proportion of Regular Army units, and for this probable reason was selected to spearhead the first sizeable American land force action. It was composed of 18 infantry regiments, five cavalry regiments, a light artillery brigade, a battalion of engineers, a Balloon detachment, and a Gatling Gun Detachment, all from

The gunboat U.S.S. *Vesuvius* terrorised Spanish ships and coastal defences, making no less than eight sortees into Santiago Harbour during June/July 1898. Her three 15 inch dynamite guns can be clearly seen in her bows. From 'Photographic History of the Spanish-American War' (1898)

the regular line, plus nine of the best prepared volunteer regiments – an aggregation of 25,000 men.[14] However, lack of time and facilities prevented Shafter from welding his Corps into a cohesive invasion force. Furthermore, the 31 transport ships sitting off Port Tampa could not accommodate his entire force, and ultimately only 819 officers and 16,058 men jammed themselves aboard the waiting vessels. The majority of the volunteers, most of the cavalry horses, many of the wheeled vehicles, and tons of baggage and equipment, were left behind.

Finally setting off from Tampa on 8 June, Shafter's truncated command began disembarkation at the small port of Daiquirí, about 17 miles east of Santiago, on 22 June. Covered by naval fire at various points along the coast, and a diversionary land attack by Cuban insurgents, the remainder of the American force had landed without opposition within three days. As soon as they were disembarked, Shafter's brigades began pushing inland on the road from Siboney towards Santiago de Cuba. Overtaking Brigadier General Henry W. Lawton's 2nd Infantry Division, advanced elements of the dismounted cavalry division under Major General Joseph Wheeler, U.S.V., fought the campaign's first engagement on 24 June at Las Guásimas, a junction of two trails about 3½ miles

inland. Deployed in two columns, eight troops of the 1st U.S. Volunteer Cavalry (also known as the 'Rough Riders'), commanded by Colonel Leonard Wood and future president Lieutenant Colonel Theodore Roosevelt, proceeded along a jungle trail on the left, while four troops each of the 1st and 10th Regular Cavalry, led by General Wheeler in company with Brigadier General Samuel Young, advanced along a road on the right.

Under orders from General Arsenio Linares Pombo, commander of the Santiago de Cuba Division, a Spanish force of approximately 2,000 men under General Antero Rubin, consisting in part of five companies of the 4th Talavera Peninsular Battalion, and three companies each of the 1st Battalion, 11th San Fernando Regiment, and the 1st Puerto Rico Provisional Battalion, lay in waiting in a strongly entrenched position on high ground. With orders to fight a rearguard action, the Spanish opened fire from their Krupp Mountain Gun detachment and smokeless

Battle of Manila Bay, painted by Alfonso Sanz. Peter Newark's Military Pictures.

Mauser rifles, and held back the American advance for about an hour. Fanning out, the American troopers groped their way foward and eventually flushed the Spaniards out of their positions, with the inexperienced 'Rough Riders' fighting as gallantly as the rest. The most memorable incident of this action was ex-Confederate General Wheeler's reaction to the ultimate Spanish withdrawal when he forgot which war he was in and, jumping up, shouted: 'Come on, boys, we got the damned Yankees on the run!'[15] This action cost 16 American dead and 52 wounded, while Spanish losses totalled about 250. Nothing now lay between Shafter's beachhead and the outer defenses of Santiago de Cuba.

Meanwhile, in Santiago Harbour, the U.S. Navy made free use of the gunboat *Vesuvius*, with its three 15 inch dynamite guns, each capable of throwing 500 pounds of explosive at a mean velocity of 185 feet per second! Between 15 June and 5 July, Lieutenant Commander John E. Pillsbury sneaked his vessel into the Harbour no less than eight times under cover of darkness in order to vent terrible destruction on the beleaguered Spanish garrison. On the first occasion,

her third salvo passed over the fort and fell among the anchored Spanish ships. A Spanish officer later told an American interrogator: 'I was thrown from my bunk by what seemed to be an earthquake... the enormous explosions damaged three ships and badly wounded 16 sailors... we feared those thunder guns with their whistling shells.' In his official report dated 22 June 1898, Admiral William Sampson stated: 'The *Vesuvius* has done almost nightly fighting... there is no doubt that the explosions of her shells have had a very important effect, especially on the morale of the enemy...'[16]

Back on land, Shafter spent the next week assembling his Army Corps near the Las Guásimas battlefield. The Spaniards meanwhile dug in on San Juan Hill, a low ridge across which the Siboney road passed before entering Santiago de Cuba. They also strengthened the fortifications at El Caney, a small village north east of the ridge on the road from Santiago to Guantánamo. Delaying his attack until his supply system could be properly established, and until troops from the second Caribbean expedition reached Cuba, Shafter thus allowed General Linares to consolidate his position unmolested. This plan was abruptly changed on 28 June, when Cuban scouts warned Shafter of the approach of 8,000 Spanish

troops from Manzanillo, a large post west of Santiago. Advised that this force would arrive no later than 3 July, Shafter determined to assault San Juan Hill at once without waiting for reinforcements.

The Fifth Corps launched its main attack against the Spanish lines east of Santiago at dawn on 1 July 1898. Shafter's plan was for General Lawton's 2nd Division to capture El Caney, believed to be held by only 500 Spanish troops, after which it would march towards Santiago on the Guantánamo road to join the 1st Division, commanded by Brigadier General Jacob F. Kent. With Wheeler's dismounted Cavalry Division in support, this force was to assault the main Spanish defences on San Juan Heights. Meanwhile, a newly arrived Volunteer brigade under General Henry M. Duffield would launch a diversionary attack along the beach toward El Morro.

The Spanish defences at El Caney comprised four wooden blockhouses, a stone fort, and a stone church which had been loopholed and converted into a blockhouse. These positions were interconnected via a system of slit trenches, and were surrounded by barbed wire. Commanded by Brigadier General

The capture of San Juan blockhouse, painted by Howard Chandler Christy in 1898. From 'The Story of the Spanish-American War and the Revolt in the Philippines,' (1898).

Joaquin Vara de Rey y Rubio, the garrison at El Caney consisted of three companies of the 1st Battalion, 29th Constitución Regiment, 40 men from the Santiago Regiment, one company of guerillas on foot, and 50 mobilised troops. The only artillery at the disposal of this force were two 8cm Plascenia Mountain Guns.[17]

The Spanish troops on San Juan Heights, under the personal command of General Linares, consisted of three companies of the 4th Talavera Battalion, one company of the 1st Puerto Rico Battalion, plus one company of volunteers. Supported by two Krupp 7.5cm Mountain Guns, this small force of about 500 men held the front line of a sector approximately one mile in length. In support were a further three companies of the Talavera Battalion, and one Mounted Guerrilla Company. These units held several blockhouses joined by slit trenches which ran along the Heights and the crest of Kettle Hill.

The events of 1 July 1898, represent the only full-scale infantry battle of the war. The assault on El Caney began at 6.30 am as Lawton's 2nd Division, consisting of Ludlow's, Miles', and Chafee's brigades, supported by Rafferty's mounted squadron of the 2nd U.S. Cavalry, advanced under the covering fire of Capron's Light Battery E, 1st Artillery Regiment. According to Shafter's plan, El Caney should have fallen within two hours, but General Del Rey and 520 Spanish troops managed to hold back about 6,600 American effectives for eight hours. According to Spanish Lieutenant José Muller, the defenders 'threw forth a hail of projectiles upon the enemy, while one company after another, without any protection, rushed with veritable fury upon the city'.[18] Finally, under close artillery support, the 12th U.S. Infantry broke into the stone fort, the main Spanish stronghold, at 3 am. Mopping up the remaining pockets of resistance took a further two hours. Del Rey and about 70 men under his command were killed during this action, while some 165 were wounded. American losses amounted to 81 killed and 360 wounded. General Linares commented later: 'When the American army attacked El Caney they had not counted on a general of Vara del Rey's stamp and on troops as fiery and inured to warfare as those he had under his command.'[19]

As a result of events at El Caney, the main American attack on San Juan Heights did not start on time. The plan of battle required Grimes' Light Battery A, 2nd Artillery Regiment, to give covering fire from 8 am whilst the dismounted Cavalry Division, now under General Samuel S. Sumner, and Kent's 1st Infantry Division, were funnelled in 100 degree heat down a narrow jungle trail and across the San Juan River swept by Spanish sniper fire and shrapnel. A U.S. Signal Corps observation balloon drew further fire as it hovered only 50 feet over the heads of the sprawling column. Shot down soon after, it contributed nothing to the action other than to add to the misery and chaos already present below.

Finally emerging at the foot of Kettle Hill and about 500 yards from the Spanish defences, advanced elements of the Cavalry Division began to form in line of battle whilst others sought desperately for cover. For an hour and a half the dismounted troopers of the 1st and 10th Regular Cavalry, with the 1st Volunteer Cavalry in their rear, were held in an exposed field of waist-high grass waiting for Kent's Infantry Division to also take up its position for the assault, and for Lawton's Division to appear on their right. Assuming command in the absence of higher ranking officers in the near vicinity, and still mounted on his war horse 'Little Texas', Lieutenant Colonel Roosevelt seized control of the situation and ordered a charge, but found a nearby Regular Captain reluctant to follow his lead. Roosevelt later recalled: 'I did not want to keep the men longer in the open suffering under a fire which they could not return. Naturally the Captain hesitated to obey this order when no word had been received from his own Colonel. So I said: "Then let my men through, sir," and rode on through the lines, followed by the grinning Rough Riders... [this] proved too much for the regulars, and they jumped up and came along, their officers and troops mingling with mine, all being delighted at the chance.'[20]

Elsewhere along the line, other elements of the Cavalry Division also began to stumble up Kettle Hill, whilst the infantry scaled the steep sides of San Juan Heights on their left. According to Richard Harding Davis, correspondent of the London *Times* who accompanied the 'Rough Riders', his comrades 'had no glittering bayonets; they were not massed in regular array. There were a few men in advance, bunched together, and creeping up a steep, sunny hill, the tops of which roared and flashed with flame. The men held their guns pressed across their breasts and stepped heavily as they climbed. Behind these first few, spreading out like a fan, were single lines of men, slipping and stumbling in the smooth grass, moving forward with difficulty, as though they were wading waist high through water, moving slowly, carefully, with strenuous effort. It was much more wonderful than any swinging charge could have been. They walked to greet death at every step, many of them, as they advanced, sinking suddenly or pitching forward and disappearing in the high grass, but the others waded on, stubbornly, forming a thin blue line that

kept creeping higher and higher up the hill. It was as inevitable as the rising tide. It was a miracle of self-sacrifice, a triumph of bull-dog courage, which one watched with breathless wonder.'[21]

Meanwhile, the Infantry Division advanced in similar fashion up San Juan Heights, initially under the covering fire of the Gatling Gun Detachment commanded by Lieutenant John H. Parker, of the 13th U.S. Infantry, and the Hotchkiss Mountain Battery of the 10th Cavalry. According to Private Charles Johnson Post, who was among those members of the 71st New York who finally joined in the attack, they 'scrambled up diagonally and clutched at tufts of the coarse grass for handholds, sometimes kicking a foothold in order to make the next step.... Just under the crest of the Hill we halted. It was entirely safe there. But above that crest the Spanish bullets were coming like hail in driving gusts.'[22] Led by the 6th and 16th Regulars, the infantrymen eventually surged over the crest, firing as they went. To their right, the Cavalry Division overran Kettle Hill, and charging across the valley between it and the northern heights, lent assistance to Kent's command. Abandoning their trenches at about 3 pm, the surviving Spaniards finally withdrew to an inner defensive ring on the outskirts of Santiago de Cuba.

These Spanish soldiers were captured at El Caney, 1 July 1898. They wear the fine-striped, or *rayadillo***, campaign uniforms and straw hats issued to most Spanish troops in Cuba.** From 'The Story of the Spanish-American War and the Revolt in the Philippines,' (1898).

The action on 1 July 1898 cost Shafter's command 205 killed and 1,177 wounded. The U.S. commander believed that his force had engaged with about 12,000 Spaniards but, in reality, less than 2,000 riflemen had held back the Fifth U.S. Army Corps for the best part of a day. The defenders also paid for their valour. The best estimates for Spanish casualties indicate a total of 595 killed, wounded, or missing. Among the former was General Linares, who died of his wounds several days after the battle.[23]

The capture of San Juan Heights brought the field campaign of the Fifth Corps to a close, and introduced them to the tedium of siege warfare. Meanwhile, the loss of San Juan Heights put the Spanish fleet at risk, and on 2 July the corps of 458 sailors assisting in the defence of the city were recalled. During the morning of the next day, Cervera took his ships out of the Harbour. What transpired was one of the worst defeats in naval history, as the entire Spanish squadron was sunk without loss to the U.S. Navy.

On the same day that Cervera put to sea, the 3,579-strong Spanish relief column from Manzanillo, under Colonel Frederico Escario Garcia, an officer on the staff of General Aldave, finally entered Santiago de Cuba from the west. During a 12-day march, Escario's column had been attacked no less than 30 times by Cuban insurgents, losing 27 dead and 71 wounded. His arrival alarmed Shafter sufficiently to prompt serious consideration of withdrawal from his recently won positions, for fear of further Spanish reinforcement cutting his supply line. These fears proving groundless. The Fifth Corps continued its investment of Santiago de Cuba and completely surrounded the city during the next few days. Several truces occurred during this period, the first from 4–5 July to permit the evacuation of women and children from the city, and the second, from 8–10 July, to discuss possible terms of surrender. General Jose Toral y Velazquez, commander of the Second Brigade, Manzanillo Division, had assumed command of the besieged city by this time, and held out for the best possible terms.

Meanwhile, the Fifh Corps continued to be dogged by supply problems, coupled with a rapidly increasing sick rate. With the onset of the rainy season, malaria and yellow fever began to ravage the American camps, and stretched the hospital accommodation at Siboney to full capacity. Concerned that Shafter might win a 'less than glorious' victory, President McKinley ordered Major General Nelson Miles to Santiago de Cuba as an observer. Arriving on 11 July, Miles was present at a further meeting with Toral two days later, on which occasion it was decided to extend the truce, and for both sides to appoint three commissioners to discuss final terms. The Americans chose two of their senior major generals, Lawton and Wheeler, plus Shafter's aide, Lieutenant John D. Miley. The Spanish delegation was led by the newly promoted Brigadier General Escario, and included the British Vice Consul, Robert Mason, who served as an interpreter.

Out of deference to the Spanish, the final terms of 'capitulation', rather than surrender, were signed on 16 July 1898. In exchange for a promise that all Spanish soldiers could return home to Spain at the expense of the United States rather than be detained as prisoners of war, plus a recommendation by the U.S. Commissioners that they could also retain their weapons, General Toral surrendered not only the 15,556 troops under his command at Santiago de Cuba, but also an additional 7,142 men at Guantanamo, Baracoa and Sagua de Tanamo. The Fifth U.S. Army Corps entered Santiago de Cuba the next day, and the war in Cuba was over.

Plans had been considered since the start of the war with Spain to invade Puerto Rico, primarily to deprive the Spanish Navy of a coaling station. With the culmination of hostilities in Cuba, Major General Miles recommended that reinforcements not now needed in fever striken Cuba should be re-assigned to an assault on Spain's other main possession in the Caribbean. With permission granted by the War Department, Miles embarked from Guantanamo Bay with what units he could gather on 21 July 1898. His newly formed Provisional Division totalled 3,415 officers and men, and included several volunteer infantry regiments, a brigade of Regular Artillery and a Provisional Battalion of recruits originally destined for the Fifth Corps.

By 1898, Puerto Rico had secured a degree of independence from Spain which had defused further attempts at insurrection. Consequently, only a token force of 7,826 Spanish and colonial soldiers garrisoned the island. With the imminent possibility of open hostilities with the U.S., a Spanish troopship carrying the Prince of Asturias Volunteer Battalion, plus two sections of mountain guns, had been successfully dispatched to the island, but a U.S. Navy blockade in place by 30 May prevented any further support from arriving.[24] After a dispute with the Navy over the choice of landing site, elements of Miles' force went ashore largely unopposed at Guancia on the southern coast of Puerto Rico on 25 July. Moving quickly east towards Ponce, Puerto Rico's second largest city, they forced the Spanish commander at that place to evacuate his forces two days later for fear of being cut off.

Thus the flood gates opened and further forces from the American First and Fifth Corps poured ashore at various points along the coast, forcing the Spanish to withdraw from the whole of the southern half of the island. In total, over 15,000 American troops landed on Puerto Rico under Miles' command, and were formed into three separate columns in readiness to invade the north. Being a master of political warfare and propaganda, Miles next issued a series of proclamations listing the rights and privileges the people of Puerto Rico would be guaranteed by the U.S. Government if they surrendered. The effect, combined with news from Cuba, was devastating to the Spanish cause, as militiamen of the local volunteer battalions refused to fight, many of them offering to act as scouts for the Americans.

Miles launched his three-pronged attack northwards on 6 August. The column under General James H. Wilson, composed of the First Division, First Corps, advanced up the military road from Ponce to San Juan, and engaged a blocking force of 400 Spaniards at Coamo three days later. Surprised by a flanking attack, the Spanish sustained 16 dead and 67 wounded, with 197 captured. American losses amounted to five wounded. Pressing on to take Coamo, the 16th Pennsylvania Infantry found the town had already surrendered to four war correspondents who had galloped into the city by mistake! Further west, the Independent Brigade, composed entirely of regulars led by General Schwan, moved from Guanica to Mayaguez and fought an action against about 1,400 Spanish troops at Hormigueros on 10 August. Spanish losses amounted to 17 killed and 56 captured, whilst American casualties were one killed and 16 wounded. Schwan's column went on to capture Mayaguez the next day.

Meanwhile, General John Brooke, with the remainder of the First Corps, proceeded from the eastern port of Arroyo north to the military road to link up with Wilson's command. Joining forces in front of the fortified town of Aibonito, this command nearly fought the most important battle of the campaign against a 1,300-strong Spanish garrison. Twenty-four hours before the main American assault

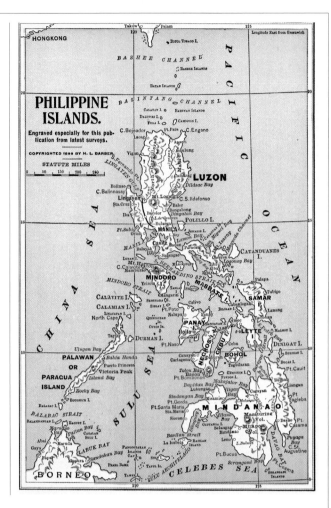

Contemporary maps of Puerto Rico and the Philippines. From Murat Halstead, 'Full Official History of the War with Spain' (1899).

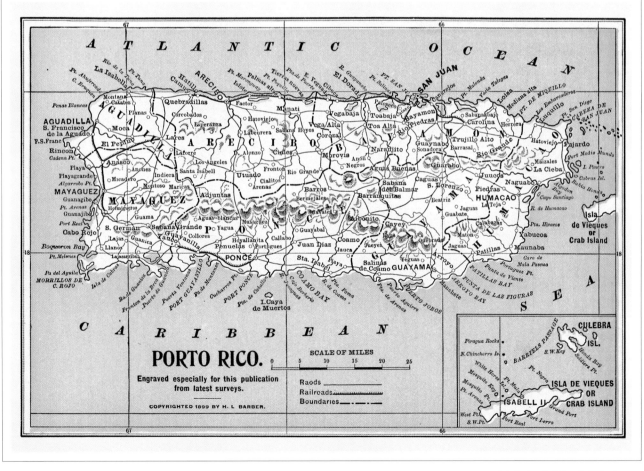

was due to begin, on 13 August, Miles was informed that a general cease fire had been arranged between Spain and the United States. With most of the island now in American hands, the Spanish agreed to cede Puerto Rico to the United States. Thus, in less than five months, the Spanish-American War had ended in the Western Hemisphere.

In the Pacific, the initial U.S. Army expedition to Manila in May, 1898, had consisted of a small force of 5,000 men whose task was to capitalise on the success of Commodore Dewey by securing the Philippine capital. Under pressure from both businessmen and politicians who wanted to expand U.S. influence in the Far East, this force was increased to 20,000 troops constituting the Eighth Army Corps, and was ordered to occupy the whole of the Philippine Archipelago. Placed under Major General Wesley Merritt, second in command of the Regular Army, it was composed of 5,000 Regulars consisting of three infantry regiments, an artillery battalion and six troops of cavalry. This force was supplemented by Volunteer infantry, cavalry and artillery units mostly from states west of the Mississippi. Towards the end of May, 1898, most of Merritt's Army Corps had assembled at San Francisco, and the 'First Expedition' set sail for Manila on 25th, arriving at Cavite on 30 June.

In the meantime, Emilio Aguinaldo, Filipino leader of the Katipunan rebellion of 1896, had returned from exile in Hong Kong on 19 May to stir up a new rebellion against Spanish rule. The revolt spread rapidly across the island of Luzon, and by early June the city of Manila was under siege with Admiral Dewey's squadron blockading the sea approaches, and the ill-equipped insurgents encircling inland.

The Spanish garrison in Manila, under Fermín Jáudenes y Alvarez, governor general in the Philippines, consisted of about 13,000 regulars and 2,000 native volunteers, who had at their disposal 22,000 weapons and an abundant supply of cartridges. This force was dug in behind a belt of forts and blockhouses containing some 92 modern artillery pieces, plus over 300 antiquated muzzleloading fortress guns. A further 11,000 Spanish troops were spread throughout some of the 7,000 other islands in the Philippines.

Upon arrival at Cavite, Merritt was accommodated in his task by Emilio Aguinaldo who graciously handed over to the American his trenches south of Manila. At the same time the U.S. commander coolly rejected Filipino suggestions of a formal alliance against Spain. Such a move was to prove unnecessary, as the Spanish general was more than willing to hand over Manila to the Americans, provided a sham battle

was staged to satisfy the honour of his country, and his garrison could surrender to U.S. forces and not to the vengeful Filipino insurgents.

Unaware due to poor communications of the armistice arranged in the Caribbean the same day, Merritt and Alvarez agreed on 12 August how long their 'battle' would last and even at what point the Spanish would surrender! Unfortunately, this information was not formally conveyed to all the combatants in both armies. Hence, at 9.35 am the next day, 8,930 American troops advanced before the appointed time of attack, which caught the Spanish defenders unawares. Shooting to kill, the U.S. infantrymen drove the Spanish from their blockhouses and into the city suburbs. The Spaniards displayed a white flag at about 11 am, but fire fights continued sporadically until late afternoon before all those involved learned of the surrender.

Disappointed at not being involved in the Battle of Manila, the Filipino nationalists grew even more angry when they were not invited to enter their own capital. The reason for their exclusion became obvious a few months later when, on 10 December 1898, the U.S. and Spain signed the Treaty of Paris which recognised Cuban independence and provided for the cession to the United States of the Philippines, Puerto Rico, and the Pacific island of Guam. Thus, in a ten-week war consisting of an unbroken series of American victories, fewer than 400 Americans were killed in battle, though more than 5,000 fell victim to tropical disease.

Two days before the final vote on the Treaty of Paris on 6 February 1899, news arrived that shots had been exchanged between jittery U.S. sentinels and Filipino soldiers. Exaggerated out of all proportions, the resulting rebellion dragged on for a further three years. To suppress it required the efforts of 70,000 American troops, of which 4,300 died. The struggle also cost the American nation $170 million.

This phase of the conflict got underway on 5 February 1899, when the divisions of General Thomas Anderson and General Arthur MacArthur charged the Filipino trenches encircling Manila, and gained control of the outer approaches to the city. One week later, MacArthur's Second Division captured the rail centre seven miles north at Caloocan. Antonio Luna, Aguinaldo's chief general, ordered his garrison to fight to the last man, and when the Americans finally overran their trenches they found dead Filipino soldiers 'stacked like cordwood'.[25] During the first two weeks of the war the Filipinos, who fought with astonishing bravery, sustained over 3,000 casualties. By the end of April 1899, General Otis extended American control some 30 miles north and east of

Manila. The rainy season during the months of May through September saw only limited activity, and a sharp deline in American military morale. During the fall, the U.S. Army launched a three-pronged assault into the central plain of Luzon which gained over 100 miles of territory, but failed in its prime objective of capturing Aguinaldo and his army.

On 12 November 1899, Aguinaldo instructed his army to abandon conventional warfare and to dissolve into guerrilla bands in order to continue the struggle. Using an elaborate underground communication network operated by a rotating company of couriers, the guerrillas exercised remarkable control over operations in the northern half of the archipelago. Their strategy was to protract the war, undermine the morale of the American army, and make the conflict so costly for the U.S. that its citizens would demand an end to hostilities. Accordingly, the guerrillas avoided open combat unless they outnumbered their adversaries, and employed 'hit and run' tactics similar to those used by the Vietcong against the same enemy nearly 70 years later. According to an insurgent broadside of the day, their policy was 'to worry the Yankee in the Pueblos occupied by them, to cut off their convoys, to cause all possible harm to their patrols, their spies and their scouts, to surprise their detachments, to crush their columns if they should pass favorable places and to exterminate traitors....'[26]

The response of the U.S. Army, by now in excess of 56,000 in the Philippines, was to occupy the whole of Luzon and beyond, imposing its presence on nearly every important island in the archipelago. In order to control this vast area, Major General MacArthur, who replaced General Otis as military governor in April 1900, ordered the construction of an extensive network of 413 outposts, each garrisoned by a small detachment whose task it was to contain a virtually invisible enemy. Sergeant Ray Hoover of Company I, 43rd U.S. Volunteer Infantry, was based at Catbalogan on Samar Island in May 1900, and wrote on the 20th of that month: 'They keep harassing the outpost every night, and yesterday they made an attack on the town, burning nearly every house, but our boys ran them into the hills.' Stationed on Leyte Island by December of that year, Hoover reported: 'My Co. and a detachment from "D" had what I would call a real fight.... Met the insurgents... about 100 riflemen and 5 to 6 hundred Bolomen [or knife carriers]. Four times they charged but each time our little band sent the lead jackets into them so fast they went back faster than they came... with the boys in khaki following them.'[27]

In March 1901, the Filipino cause was dealt a fatal blow with the capture of Emilio Aguinaldo by a troop of the 3rd U.S. Cavalry and a battalion of 300 Maccabebe scouts. Despite a proclamation from their leader urging his people to surrender, issued on 19 April 1901, thousands of freedom fighters vowed to continue the struggle to the death. On 28 September, hundreds of bolo-wielding Filipinos rushed without warning into Balangiga, on Samar Island, and hacked to death 38 members of Company C, 9th U.S. Infantry. The 'Balangiga Massacre' caused the U.S. Army to step up its efforts in order to stamp out the last pockets of resistance in the Philippines.

Finally, on 4 July 1902, President Theodore Roosevelt announced an end to the 'Philippine Insurrection'. A total of 126,500 Americans took up 'the White Man's burden' and saw action in the Philippines, with a peak strength of 70,000 men at any single time. Of these, over 4,200 were killed, while about 2,800 were wounded, at a financial cost of over $400 million. This resulted in a human casualty rate of 5.5 per cent, and represents one of the highest rates of American loss in any war in the history of the United States. The Filipinos suffered far greater battle losses amounting to between 16,000-20,000 killed, plus a further 200,000 deaths from disease, famine, and other war-related causes. During the years that followed, the U.S. found the Philippines to be a disappointing prize. The islands did not, as expected, develop into a centre for Oriental trade, but came to be regarded rather as a military liability.

U.S. Forces

A victim of repeated cuts in Federal government spending since the Civil War, the U.S. Regular Army in 1897 had an authorised strength of only 2,143 officers and 26,040 men, which was insufficient even to keep its 25 infantry, ten cavalry and five artillery regiments at their minimum peace time capacity. In reality, two companies of each infantry and cavalry regiment existed purely on paper, and the officers assigned to them were dispersed to inspect National Guard summer encampments and to teach military science at land-grant colleges. The properly manned battalions and companies were scattered across the continent in over 70 small military posts where they functioned mainly as a police force against rebellious Native Americans or striking labourers. In any case, federal law forbade the maintainence in peacetime of any troop formation larger than a regiment, and only rarely were whole regiments assembled at a single post. By 1896 a total of 77 posts were held by three or more military companies.[28] As relationships deteriorated with Spain at the beginning of 1898, this comparatively small regular army was mobilised for war. On 15 April, 22 infantry regiments were ordered to assemble at three ports on the Gulf of Mexico, while six cavalry regiments and most of the artillery were directed into camp in northern Georgia.

With the possibility of war with Spain looming ever larger, it was the original intention of the McKinley Administration to raise an all-regular army of 100,000 men to invade Cuba. To this end, U.S. Congress took important measures on 8 March 1898, to increase its Regular Army by authorising two new artillery regiments – the 6th and the 7th. Following this, Republican congressman from Iowa, John A. T. Hull, introduced a bill to enlarge the Regular Army to a wartime strength of 104,000 men by increasing to a prescribed maximum the enlisted strength of every infantry company, cavalry troop and artillery battery. But this measure did not appeal to the militia or citizen soldiers of the nation who believed that any such enlargement would represent a first step towards militarism, and the loss of their cherished freedoms. Under continued pressure from the National Guard lobby, the McKinley Administration eventually gave up its plans for an all-regular wartime army, and agreed to a compromise. On 22 April 1898, Congress authorised the President to raise a temporary Volunteer force of 125,000 men – the approximate strength of the National Guard – to serve for two years or for the duration of hostilities with Spain, whichever was shorter.

Once the National Guard had been placated, Congress increased the statutory size of the regular army on 26 April 1898 to 64,719 officers and men. This was achieved by enlarging units already in existence. Infantry regiments were changed into 12-company, three-battalion organisations by reviving their dormant companies and creating two new ones. The size of an infantry company was increased to 106 other ranks, which consisted of one first sergeant, one quartermaster sergeant, four sergeants, 12 corporals, two musicians, one artificer, one wagoner and 84 privates. A cavalry troop was permitted 100 enlisted men; an artillery battery was increased in size from 173 to 200 men; and an engineer company to 150.

However, recruitment was hampered by the competing attractions of the Volunteer service, and the Regular Army could not fill its ranks swiftly enough to monopolise planned offensive operations against Spain. When presented with the choice, most recruits preferred to enlist in Volunteer units where they expected to serve with friends under less strict discipline. Hundreds of Regular officers were also attracted to leave their posts encouraged by the prospect of promotion within a Volunteer regiment. By the end of May 1898, the Regular Army had enlisted only 8,500 of the 36,000 men required to reach its expanded wartime strength. Hence, most Regular units left the U.S. on active service before their recruits could join them, and commenced operations against the Spanish with less than half their prescribed number.

As the Army began to mass in large Federal camps such as Chickamauga Park, Georgia, and Camp Alger, Virginia, it was organised in to army corps, each of which at full strength contained 30,000 men in three divisions. Each division consisted of three brigades and each brigade of three regiments. An army corps contained only infantry, whilst artillery and cavalry were assigned to independent formations which could be attached to corps during campaigns. As a result of General Orders of 7 and 16 May, seven army corps were created, with a major general appointed to command each. An eighth corps was established on 21 June. They were organised and saw service as follows:

Corps	Cantonment	Operations
First	Chickamauga	Puerto Rico Campaign, plus elements to Philippines
Second	Camp Alger	Elements to Puerto Rico and Philippines
Third	Chickamauga	Elements involved in occupation of Cuba
Fourth	Tampa	Elements to Puerto Rico, and later Cuban occupation
Fifth	Tampa	Santiago Campaign
Sixth	Chickamauga	Never raised
Seventh	Jacksonville	Occupation of Havana after the armistice
Eighth	San Francisco	Philippine Campaign and occupation of Hawaii

The Sixth Corps, for reasons never explained, remained unmanned much to the chagrin of its commander, General James H. Wilson, who was convinced he was the victim of a War Department plot. Of the organised corps, the Fifth, designated the responsibility of invading Cuba, was composed largely of Regulars. The Eighth Corps contained a mixture of Regulars and Volunteers. The Fourth Corps included a few Regular units. The other four corps were composed entirely of Volunteers.

With the war against Spain over, and U.S. forces committed to a long struggle in the Philippines, President McKinley signed a bill on 2 March 1899 which authorised the Regular Army to continue at its wartime strength of 65,000 men. Each infantry regiment was to consist of '1 Colonel, 1 Lieutenant-Colonel; 3 Majors; 14 Captains, two of whom shall be available for detail as Adjutant and Quartermaster; 16 1st Lieutenants, of whom 1 shall be... Commissary and 3... Battalion Adjutants; 12 2nd Lieutenants; 1 Sergeant Major; 1 Quartermaster Sergeant; 1

Artist Frederic Remington accompanied the U.S. Fifth Corps to Cuba in June 1898, and left a vivid account of his experiences in both paintings and sketches. His 'U.S. Infantryman armed with Krag-Jörgensen magazine rifle', produced in 1901, captures the appearance of the typical 'doughboy' who scaled San Juan Heights on 1 July 1898. Peter Newark's Military Pictures.

Commissary Sergeant...; 3 Battalion Sergeant Majors...; 1 band [consisting of 28 musicians], and 12 companies, organized into 3 battalions of 4 companies each...' Each cavalry regiment was to consist of the same field and staff as per infantry, with the following

Ray Hoover was born at Philippi, West Virginia, in 1876, and enlisted in the 17th U.S. Infantry on 7 June 1898. He served in Cuba and Puerto Rico, and was honourably discharged with the rank of corporal on 14 April 1899. Re-enlisting in Co. I, 43rd U.S. Volunteer Infantry during the following October, he served in the Philippines from January 1900 until 1904, being promoted to command a specialist native outfit organised in May 1901 called the Philippines Scouts, with the rank of 2nd Lieutenant. He is seen here in his khaki officer's uniform, including the Model 1899 blouse with light blue shoulder straps, plain standing collar and cuffs, and officer's sword belt fastened by the regulation gilt belt plate bearing the 'Arms of the United States' encircled by a silver laurel wreath. U.S. Army Military History Institute/courtesy of Ron Beifuss. Photo by Jim Enos.

This Volunteer in full marching order, and armed with a 'Trapdoor' Springfield rifle, appears to be wearing the canvas fatigue suit of brown cotton duck which was issued in large numbers to U.S. forces in Cuba, Puerto Rico and the Philippines, in lieu of khaki cotton drill uniforms at the beginning of the war. He also carries a 'horse-collar blanket roll', which contained half a 'shelter tent'. From Murat Halstead, 'Full Official History of the War with Spain' (1899).

additions and differences: '2 Veterinarians... 3 Squadron Sergeant Majors... and 12 troops organized into three squadrons of 4 troops each...' Each regiment of artillery was to be composed of '4 batteries, of which 2 may be organized as field artillery.' The 6th and 7th Regiments were also created at this time.[29]

To ensure sufficient manpower to pacify the Philippines, the bill also authorised an additional force of 35,000 federally controlled volunteers to serve for 'two years and four months, unless sooner discharged'.

This led to the creation of the 26th through 49th U.S. Volunteer Infantry, and the 11th and 12th U.S. Volunteer Cavalry. Two of these new units – the 36th and 37th Infantry – were largely composed of veterans of state volunteer regiments who agreed to remain in the Philippines to finish the fight. The 48th and 49th Infantry were composed of African Americans.

The unexpected call for 125,000 volunteers in April 1898, followed by a further appeal in May, found the U.S. Quartermaster's Department with their clothing stock piles capable of catering only for a three-month period for the 28,000-man peacetime Regular Army, plus an additional 8,000 to 10,000 men. The Department had on hand at its depots or due on contract about 28,000 blouses, 53,000 undress caps, 28,000 campaign hats, 47,000 dark blue shirts, 35,000 pairs of trousers and 23,000 pairs for mounted men,

12,000 ponchos, 69,000 blankets, and 62,000 pairs of shoes.[30] During mid-March 1898, Quartermaster General Marshall Ludington had ordered his depots to accelerate the production of clothing, whilst he surveyed market conditions for the supply of greater amounts of materials. However, he did not issue large contracts for uniform cloth and tent canvas until 20 and 25 April. Nonetheless, by the 30th of that month, the Quartermaster's Department was in a position to clothe an additional 25,000 men.

Assured of funding by Congress amounting to $130 million, the clothing bureaus lost no time in redressing the situation. During peacetime they were accustomed to manufacturing most supplies in their own workshops using semi-finished or raw materials purchased from private contractors. Faced with huge demands, the Department hired additional workers and installed new machinery, such as the electric cutting and stitching machines which supplemented the hand sewing of uniforms for the first time at the clothing plant in Philadelphia.

Drastic though these measures were, they proved insufficient to meet the needs of the war-swollen army, and the Quartermaster's Department was required to make large contracts with private companies in order to secure sufficient cloth. Indeed, General Ludington reported: 'The kerseys and flannels of standard quality used for making army blouses and trousers were not to be had in the market, and it was necessary to have them manufactured.'[31] He quickly discovered that only a few firms were capable of manufacturing Army uniform fabrics, which were generally heavier and more durable than civilian goods. To meet immediate demands, he ordered his purchasing officers to buy up all the cloth that approached the colour and quality stipulated in Army regulations. One immediate result was the purchase of a lighter weight, dark blue fabric, instead of regulation sky blue kersey, for trousers.[32]

The depots at Philadelphia, Chicago, Boston, Saint Louis and Jeffersonville in Indiana all acted as purchasing agencies, whilst additional depots were opened in other major cities to tap a wider market. The office established at San Francisco purchased on

These U.S. Regular infantrymen encamped in Florida display the full range of fatigue uniform before the adoption of khaki field dress. Four men wear the five-button blouse, or sack coat, whilst the others look more comfortable in their dark blue overshirts. Note the corporal in the rear with white chevron and trouser seam stripes. Two men wear Mills cartridge belts, which probably denote their Regular Army status. From 'Photographic History of the Spanish-American War' (1898).

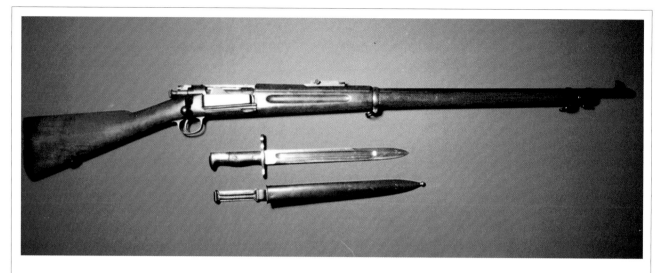

Above.

The Model 1898 Krag-Jörgensen rifle and bayonet. This weapon was produced at the Springfield Arsenal, and was the standard issue long arm of the U.S. Regular Army. It was later issued to many Volunteer units.

Left.

Breech with loading gate open.

Left below.

Breech with loading gate closed.

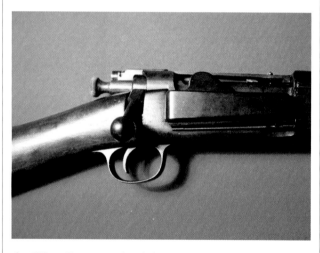

of 30 April and 5 May which required the quartermaster of each Volunteer regiment, as soon as it entered federal service, to determine the amount of state supplies the unit possessed and how much additional material would be required from the federal government. These officers would next requisition the additional clothing, arms and accoutrements from the War Department, who then dispatched whatever was needed to the state camps. The federal authorities also give the state governments receipts for all National Guard property taken into Volunteer service, and would subsequently reimburse the states in cash or in kind.

This cumbersome system plus an inefficient process of distribution, resulted in many Volunteer regiments flooding into camp ill-equipped for active service. As late as 4 June 1898, Major General Nelson A. Miles, commanding the camp at Tampa, reported that several units had arrived 'without uniforms... some without blankets, tents, or camp equipage'. Nelson added: 'To illustrate the embarrassment caused by present conditions, 15 [railroad] cars loaded with uniforms were side-tracked 25 miles away from Tampa, and remained there for weeks while the troops were suffering for clothing.'[33] In an attempt to circumvent at least some of these delays, General Ludington delegated full contracting powers to his

the West Coast much of the clothing used by the Manila Expedition. On most occasions purchasing officers called for bids on major supply orders. Dependent on circumstances, manufacturers were given from 24 hours to 10 days to respond by sending to the depot quartermaster samples of goods offered. After inspection, these were sent to Washington accompanied by a recommendation of the reward of a contract, which was almost invariably ratified by the Quartermaster General.

This time-consuming process was further confounded by the War Department's general orders subordinates within his department later in the war. Using these increased powers, depot quartermasters awarded contracts to the lowest bidder – thereby securing goods of the best possible quality and generally at pre-war prices. In total, the Quartermaster's Department acquired about two-thirds of its clothing via private sources.

During the three and a half months war period beginning 1 May and ending 15 August 1898, the Quartermaster's Department was reported to have purchased or contracted for the following number of articles: *(list on next page)*

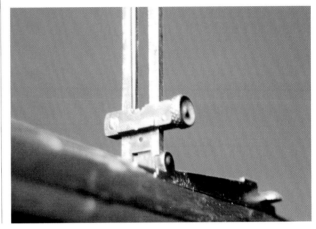

Top right.
Reverse side of breech. Note the cartouche mark on the wooden stock showing '1899' as the date of production.

Right.
Upright leaf on the rear sight.

Below.
Model 1896 bayonet.

Bottom.
Bayonet scabbard with metal frog which hooked over the belt.

Photos by the author/ courtesy of Kurt Hughes.

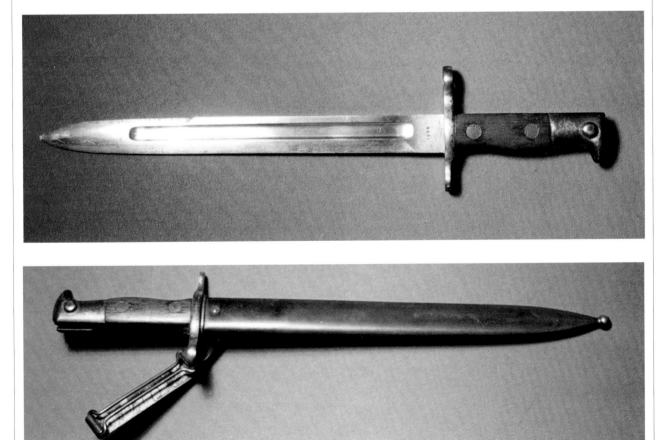

Forage caps	230,000
Blouses	274,232
Field and summer uniforms	153,169
Canvas, fatigue coats	31,601
Canvas fatigue trousers, pairs	50,000
Hats, campaign	476,705
Shirts, dark blue flannel	548,634
Leggins	588,800
Overcoats	129,000
Ponchos, rubber	325,385
Shoes, barrack, pairs	76,093
Shoes, calfskin, pairs	782,303
Stockings, cotton, pairs	1,996,699
Stockings, woolen, pairs	150,942
Blankets	546,338

Despite this achievement, a number of volunteers recorded how woefully inefficient the uniform supply system was at the beginning of the conflict. In June 1898, an anonymous officer at Camp St. Thomas in Florida commented: 'When clothing was supplied there were no shoes and no undershirts, and hats of only one size 7⅜ – which, save in a few cases, came down over the heads of the men and rested on their ears, which gave the troops a sufficiently picturesque appearance, something like a mardi gras parade. The trousers were only about half enough to go round. No rubber coats were furnished – so absolutely necessary as protection against tropical rains – and so the men who could do so bought them for themselves. I am still wearing a borrowed hat... and as to these leggins, I got a private soldier to draw them for me.'[34]

Charles Johnson Post, who enlisted in the 71st New York Volunteers during May 1898 recalled: 'I had always thought that a "blouse" was specifically an article of feminine apparel, a sort of loose shirtwaist with a snappy, come-hither effect. But in that man's army, a blouse was anything worn outside a shirt and inside an overcoat, and instantly provocative of a sergeant's acute anguish if it was unbuttoned. Also, it was supposed to fit. They were short on blouses when mine was issued; that is, short of normal blouses for normal men. So my blouse was left over from some outsized predecessor, a mere fragment of whose clothing would have oufitted me inside and out, with a Sunday suit left over. The turned-back sleeves reached my elbows; the blouse folded around me so that its buttons were at all times under my arms, and it reached to my knees like a frock coat.' Post had fonder memories of his trousers, which he described as being 'cerulean-blue pants with a broad, deep-blue stripe down the sides, and they fitted reasonably well'.[35]

Many of the 'blouses', more correctly called sack coats, issued to volunteers in 1898 began to change colour due to inferior dyes and poor quality of manufacture. In a short period of time, numerous variations of blue, purple and even green resulted, giving the troops a motley appearance. The quartermaster in San Francisco returned the coats of 10 out of 12 companies of the 1st Tennessee Volunteers which he judged to be so 'shoddy' they would have disgraced even 'the property of a ten-cent show'.[36] Frederick Funston, commanding the 20th Kansas in May 1898, recalled: 'The spectacle the troops made after the dye began to fade, which it did in a few weeks, would have been laughable if it had not been so maddening to those most concerned. But the new clothing was warm, and answered a good purpose until it could be replaced by better.'[37] The Quartermaster's Department did indeed replace these uniforms with those of a standardised and more substantial quality as quickly as possible.

Based on the firm conviction that the use of light woolen fabrics was more conducive to the preservation of health in warm climates, the Department had not issued warm weather uniforms to the U.S. Army since 1850. This belief was further re-inforced by experiments conducted by medical officers of the French Army in Africa during the 1870s. Hence, renewed requests for a summer uniform for the post-Civil War U.S. Army found little support among Quartermaster officers.[38] Troops serving in the South and Southwestern States reluctantly continued to wear the regulation blue wool suit with minor modifications. Indeed, in August 1897, a soldier wrote home: 'It is high time the government issued an unlined blouse for summer wear. No one feels the need of it more than the poor enlisted men who are sweltering these hot days in the same blouse that is issued in the Dakotas during the most extreme cold weather.'[39] With their needs still not met by 1898, the U.S. Fifth Corps embarked on the Cuban campaign in the same woolen uniforms. Sitting on a hillside watching the marching columns leaving Daiquirí, artist Frederic Remington observed that the sides of the road were 'blue with cast-off uniforms. Coats and overcoats were strewn about, while the gray blankets lay in the camps just where the soldiers had gotten up from them after the night's rest.'[40]

The nearest clothing to a light-weight summer outfit supplied by the U.S. Army before the war with Spain was a canvas fatigue suit of cotton duck dyed brown, similar to the working clothes worn by miners in the western states, which first saw service in 1883. This was followed in 1897 by a bleached version using similar material, suitable for service in extreme southern latitudes. On the recommendation of General Miles, and in lieu of anything else more suitable, the Quartermaster's Department adopted a variation of the former brown uniform during early April 1898. On 11 June, the *Army and Navy Journal* was able to report: 'This week the deliveries of canvas clothing for the Cuban and Philippine Island campaigns began.' By 18 June, the Quartermaster's Department stated that 25,739 canvas coats and trousers, and 23,959 canvas hats, had been produced.[41] Despite these reports, distribution of the brown canvas uniform was very slow. Delivery to the camps in the South, such as Chickamauga and Tampa, suffered when, as observed earlier, the railroad cars containing them were parked in a siding and forgotten for weeks while the troops suffered. Due to congestion in the port of Siboney, little if any of this clothing reached Shafter's troops in Cuba until after the Spanish had surrendered.

Towards the end of July 1898, some units were reported to be in receipt of canvas outfits of brown cotton duck construction. On the 26th of that month, the First Battalion of the 1st U.S. Volunteer Engineers, commanded by Colonel Griffin, had 'khaki uniforms'.[42] Three days later, Colonel T. H. Barber, 1st New York Volunteers, was advised that 'uniforms for the Tropics' would be issued to his regiment on arrival at San Francisco.[43] Most of the regiments assigned to the invasion of Puerto Rico wore the canvas suits. By the end of August, Secretary of War Russell A. Alger could report that 83,200 canvas uniforms had been issued.[44]

In the meantime, to meet objections to the unsuitability of heavy woolen uniforms in the tropics, Ludington ordered the weight of the kersey for sky blue trousers to be reduced from 22 to 16 ounces, had linings removed from woolen flannel sack coats, and furnished summer underwear. More importantly, he contracted for the manufacture of an experimental lot of 10,000 tropical uniforms made from khaki, a closely woven, light-weight brown cotton drill of the type used with great success by the British Army. He also tried to place orders for larger amounts of the same cloth, only to encounter frustrating delays. American

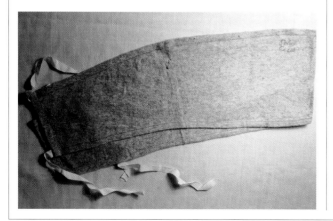

Top.
The 1885-pattern drab canvas haversack, used by U.S. infantrymen and dismounted cavalrymen during the Spanish-American War and Philippines Insurrection. They were usually marked with the owner's name.

Middle top.
Interior showing the knife, fork, and spoon sheaths, made from scrap leather, placed in their pockets. Photos by the author/ courtesy of Kurt Hughes.

Middle bottom.
The oblate spheroid tin canteen. The unit designation stencilled on the drab duck cover indicates that this one was carried by enlisted man number 19 of Company C, 20th U.S. Infantry. Note the brass hooks passing through the wire loops soldered either side of the body of the canteen. Photo by the author/ courtesy of Kurt Hughes.

Bottom.
An abdominal bandage. By mid-1899, two of these were issued per man supposedly to ward off yellow fever and other tropical diseases. Photo by the author/ courtesy of Kurt Hughes.

firms had little experience weaving and dyeing this kind of fabric. Hence, depot quartermasters rejected a number of bids on substantial lots of brown cotton drill material because the samples of fabric were of such inferior quality. It was not until 8 June that the New York depot quartermaster, being satisfied with the cloth offered, felt able to issue contracts for 50,000 suits of khaki cotton uniforms. Meanwhile in Manila, Chief Quartermaster James W. Pope met the need for light-weight clothing by purchasing khaki and white summer uniforms of sufficient quality made from local cloth.[45]

Nonetheless, tropical uniforms received by the majority of U.S. troops during the first year of conflict continued to be of inferior quality, and lacked strength due to various efforts to produce very light weight garments. In Cuba during the summer of 1898, Major General of Volunteers, Inspector General J.C. Breckenridge commented: 'The Kahki *[sic]* quickly loses its shape and dandy color, and is not strong enough to withstand thorns.'[46] As late as 1 July 1899, Major General Elwell S. Otis, commanding the U.S. Eighth Corps in Manila, advised the Adjutant General's Office in Washington, D.C. via telegraph: 'Khaki uniform United States, defective material and workmanship, unfit for issue; should not be sent. Uniform of excellent quality procured here at Manila.'[47] In fact, Otis had been obtaining 'light quality' clothing at Manila, and from Hong Kong, since September, 1898. The following February he informed Adjutant General H.C. Corbin: 'Have contracts with Shanghai and Hongkong houses for 50,000 khaki uniforms, 20,000 to be delivered in March, rest within four months; have 10,000 white uniform suits delivered. No khaki or white uniforms required from the United States...' In response, Corbin advised: 'That will be corrected hereafter... Continue purchases to meet wants [for] six months, by which time it is believed... [that] satisfactory khaki clothing can be placed [in] Manila from here.'[48]

Top right.
A standard quart-sized U.S. Army tin cup of the type used between 1874 and 1901, and usually suspended from the haversack.

Right.
Note the 'U.S.' stamped ⅜ inch-high letters on the handle.
Photo by the author/ courtesy of Dusan Farrington.

Bottom left.
Front of an 1878-pattern drab canvas U.S. infantry blanket bag.

Bottom right.
Rear of bag. Note how the leather carrying straps were wider at that part which went over the shoulder for greater comfort.

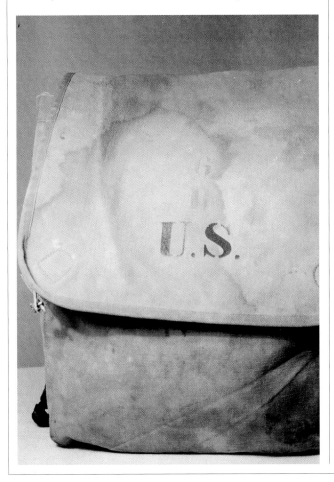

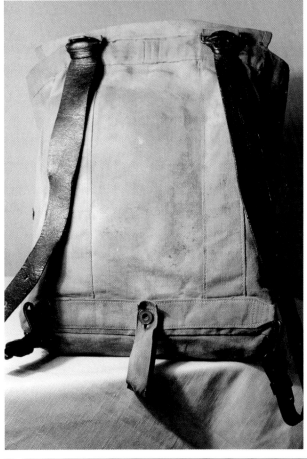

A camp photograph of General Miles and staff which displays the complete array of undress and field dress worn by general officers and staff during the Spanish-American War. Miles, seated third from the right, wears the unlikely combination of M1895 sack coat, dark blue trousers, and white summer helmet. His white gauntlets are regulation. Major General Joseph Wheeler, commander of the cavalry division of the Fifth Army Corps in 1898, is seated fourth from right wearing a M1898 dark blue blouse with the top three buttons undone. This garment appears to have at least two lower pockets. Three men wear the khaki field dress adopted for officers on 9 May 1898. That worn by the man stood at the centre shows the regulation facings on the collar, shoulder straps, and cuffs. The others wear a mixture of M1895 coats and M1898 blouses with their campaign hats. From 'Photographic History of the Spanish-American War' (1898).

Despite these efforts, the Quartermaster Department consistently failed to produce a standardised khaki-coloured field service uniform, or to overcome problems caused by fading. Hence, by 1902 they began to turn to olive drab woollen clothing for colder climates. By 12 July, 1909, they were issuing uniforms of olive drab cotton via Specification No. 850, and the days of 'American' khaki were done! [49]

Nonetheless, during the Cuban/Philippines conflict the Quartermaster's Department continued its efforts to acquire khaki cloth in sufficient quantity, and to develop a comfortable yet durable tropical uniform. At the beginning of May 1899, bids were opened in New York for 300,000 yards of khaki to be made into 50,000 suits for 'the troops in Manila'. At the same time, Colonel Patten, Assistant Quartermaster in Washington, D.C., listed the complete uniform by then available for the Regular troops in the Philippines, should they see fit to spend $28.35 of their clothing account on it: 'An unlined blouse, two khaki suits, two pairs of Berlin gloves for parade duty, a cork helmet, a pair of leggings, a poncho blanket, two light weight shirts, a pair of barrack shoes, a pair of russet shoes, three pairs of light weight cotton stockings, two white duck suits, a pair of trousers of sixteen ounce kersey, two cotton undershirts, two wool undershirts, two outershirts of gingham or chambray, two pairs of jean drawers, two nankeen shirts, two abdominal bandages, one mosquito bar and one mosquito head net.' [50]

Regarding shoes procured at the outbreak of hostilities, many pairs did not conform to the army shoe adopted in January 1898, which was made of 'lighter calfskin, upon lasts conforming more closely to the anatomy of the human foot'. According to the report

Major General Nelson A. Miles, Commander of the United States Army in 1898, in full dress frock coat with two rows of nine regulation buttons arranged in groups of three, denoting the rank of major general. He has chosen to wear his buff silk net sash across his body as well as around his waist. His sword belt was of red Russian leather with three stripes of gold embroidery. From Murat Halstead, 'Full Official History of the War with Spain'.

of General Ludington published in December of that year: 'The urgency of the situation made it necessary to procure a large number of shoes at once, and as the newly adopted Army shoe could not be procured in sufficient quantity, it was found absolutely necessary to purchase such shoes as could be had in the market, conforming approximately to the standard Army shoe in pattern and quality.' He concluded that 'these shoes were found good and serviceable', but suggested that machine-sewing soles had caused problems.[51]

Major General Thomas M. Anderson and staff, in command of the 1st Division, 8th Army Corps, at Manila. General Anderson stands fourth from the left wearing a double-breasted M1898 field dress blouse. Two other officers wear the single-breasted version of this blouse, while the remainder pose in M1895 undress sack coats trimmed with black mohair braid. From 'Photographic History of the Spanish American War' (1898).

At the outbreak of the Spanish-American War, there were also problems arming the vastly expanded American army. The main longarm of the Regular Army was the 30-calibre, five-shot Krag-Jörgensen. Adopted in 1893 after extensive weapon tests by the Ordnance Department, and in the face of an uproar of public protest at the adoption of a foreign design, this was the first general-issue magazine arm used by the U.S. Regular Army. The Krag-Jörgensen rifle was developed between 1886–1889 at Kongsberg Vapenfabrik, the Norwegian state arsenal, by Ole H. Krag and Erik Jörgensen. The most characteristic feature of this small bore weapon was its magazine which lay horizontally under the receiver. It was loaded by opening a loading gate on the right side of the rifle and inserting loose cartridges. The magazine follower and spring were part of the gate and were compressed when the loading gate was opened, and released when it was closed. Cartridges were forced sideways and up a ramp and fed into the action from the lower left hand side. The design also included a very simple magazine cut-off, which facilitated a single loaded round to be fired.[52]

The first 'Krag' issued to the U.S. Army was the M1892 version, known as the U.S. Rifle, Cal. 30, which reached the troops in 1894. About 25,000 M1892s were produced at the Springfield Arsenal. This weapon had a 30 inch barrel and weighed 9.3 pounds. Its walnut stock was a straight-grip pattern, whilst its handguard extended from the receiver ring to the barrel band. The front sight was a narrow blade and the rear sight consisted of an open U notch which was adjustable from 300 to 600 yards on a stepped

Bottom left.
A khaki blouse of the type prescribed for general officers and officers of the general staff, corps, and departments on 9 May 1898. The 'dark sky-blue' woollen facings on this blouse were made from the same material as that used for general officers' full dress trousers. This example has the unofficial facing colour on the pocket flaps.

Bottom right.
Note the two-inch wide box plait running down the back.

Right.
The collar was closed by two hooks and eyes, and the front was fastened by five large regulation gilt 'eagle' buttons.
Photos by the author/courtesy of Kurt Hughes.

ramp, and a fold up leaf adjustable up to 1,900 yards. Issued with the Krag rifle was a knife style bayonet with a 12 inch blade.

As with any new rifle, minor problems cropped up which necessitated small changes being made to the M1892 Krag. So many modifications were introduced within the first two years of U.S. service that it was decided to give the weapon a new model number. Thus, the M1896 rifle, used by most U.S. regulars and many Volunteers in the Spanish-American War, was born. The most obvious changes to this weapon were external, and included the scrapping of the cleaning rod under the barrel, which was replaced with a three piece rod carried in the butt trap. The rear sight was

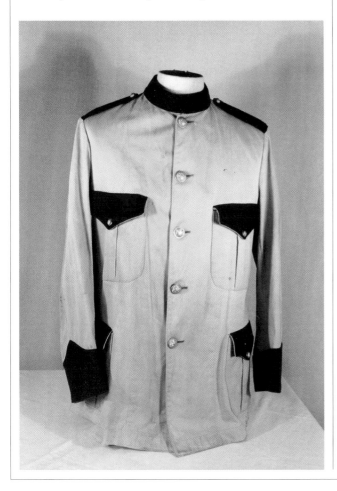

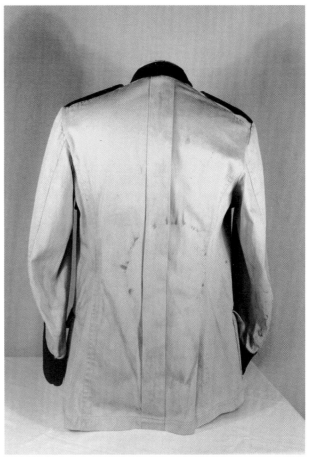

altered from a stepped to a smooth tangent which was adjustable from 300 to 650 yards, whilst the upright leaf was adjustable from 700 to 1,800 yards. Also the rifle's muzzle was crowned and the heel of the buttstock was curved. In total, about 62,000 M1896 Krag rifles were produced at the Springfield Arsenal, and most M1892s were upgraded to M1896 specifications when returned for repairs.

Two years later further changes led to the creation of the M1898 rifle. Most of the modifications to this weapon were concerned with the magazine cut-off and the rear sight. The cut-off lever was altered so that the rifle functioned as a single loader when the lever was turned down, as opposed to up, as it had been on the '92 and '96 models. This alteration was made in the belief that when the lever was up in 'repeater' position, it would be more obvious to officers and squad leaders who could thus more closely maintain fire control and avoid excessive expenditure of ammunition. Several different rear sights underwent experimentation following the introduction of the M1898. The Dickson-pattern sight used on that model was a tangent-style sight with a U notch, adjustable from 200 to 2,000 yards. This made allowances for windage, and was graduated to cater for the new high velocity .30-40 cartridge. The M1901, or Buffington, sight was also adjustable for windage and had a wide V notch adjustable from 100 to 500 yards. Its fold up leaf permitted the marksman to use either an aperture or V notch adjustable from 100 to 2,000 yards. This sight was introduced when the high velocity cartridge was withdrawn. Finally, the M1902 sight, another Dickson design, was similar to the M1898 pattern, but had a small plate with an aperture attached which could be moved up for use instead of the U notch.

According to General D. W. Flagler, Chief of Ordnance, 'some 30,000 magazine [Krag] rifles' had been produced at the Springfield Arsenal up to 30 June 1898. By 13 August, a total of 370 were being made per day by 'working double shifts of men'.[53] An approximate total of 324,000 M1898 Krag rifles had been produced before production was halted in 1904.

Several models of Krag-Jörgensen carbine were adopted to arm the U.S. regular cavalry during the 1890s. The first was the Model 1896, which had a 22 inch barrel and a half stock with a saddle ring on the left side of the wrist. The rear sight was mounted just behind the barrel band, and had an extension on top to protect the sight when it was slid into the saddle scabbard. A total of 22,500 M1896 carbines had been manufactured by 1899.

The Model 1898 Krag carbine was designed specifically for the .30-40 high velocity cartridge. When that round was found to be too powerful for the weapon's action, production ceased after only about 5,000 of this model were made. The Model 1899 Krag carbine had a stock with a longer fore-end, and a hand guard which protruded sufficiently to protect the rear sight from the saddle scabbard. Some of the early M1899 weapons had a headless cocking piece in order to shorten the lock time of the Krag's firing pin. Considered to be the last traditional 'cavalry' carbine, about 36,000 of this model were made before production finally halted in 1904.[54]

In order to encourage a uniform, if obsolescent, arming of state forces, Secretary of War Alger had obtained Congressional permission in 1897 for late-model 'Trapdoor' Springfield rifles, discarded by the Regulars after over 20 years service in favour of the Krag-Jörgensen, to be made available from Federal stock piles. In return for other weapons handed in, most National Guard thus found themselves in possession of this single-shot breechloader which used charcoal powder to propel a .45 calibre soft lead bullet. The Volunteers were also subsequently armed with this weapon. Although it was readily available, the disadvantage of charcoal powder ammunition was that it created clouds of smoke which exposed the troops' positions to the enemy when they fired. Indeed, on 9 July 1898, General Shafter reported to Washington on its service in Cuba: 'The use of black powder instantly brought volleys against regiments using Springfield [rifles], and was very demoralising on those regiments.'[55] Private Post of the 71st New York recalled: 'With the first blast from our black-powder .45-70 Springfields, the front was clouded in an instantaneous white fog... You jammed a cartridge in, snapped the butt... hard against your shoulder – for the recoil was like a hurled brick – and pulled the trigger. The Spaniards instantly turned all they had into our cloud of smoke, including their Maxim machine guns.'[56]

To counter this, the Ordnance Department developed a smokeless cartridge for use with the Springfield which contractors were requested to begin manufacturing as soon as possible. As there were only two establishments in the U.S. capable of producing smokeless powder at that time, and both of these owned patents on the process, supply was slow. Also, despite efforts by the Ordnance Bureau to increase production of the Krag for more widespread use, volunteers saw extensive action in both Cuba and the Philippines predominantly using black powder ammunition.

Some volunteer regiments, and particularly those

involved in the invasion of Puerto Rico, were issued with Krag rifles. On 21 July, General Miles telegraphed Secretary of War Alger: 'I hope you will order enough 30-caliber rifles sent to Porto Rico [sic] by first steamer to arm Sixth Massachusetts, Sixth Illinois, and all other regiments that have started with Springfields...; also put 30-caliber rifles in hands of troops before they leave, with belts and ammunition.'[57] Furthermore, on the same date, Alger advised General Shafter in Cuba to supply the volunteers under his command with arms captured from the Spanish. Shafter responded the next day: 'I think I can arm the volunteers with Mauser rifles; about 5,000 or 6,000 Spanish Mausers; about the same number Mauser Argentina and Remington.'[58] Twelve days later, General Miles recommended that the manufacture of Springfield rifles be discontinued as they were 'obsolete, and should not be a part of the army equipment'.[59]

Nonetheless, the weapon continued in service. The Ames Sword Company, of Chicopee, Massachusetts, was working on an order for 50,000 blued-steel bayonet scabbards 'to be fitted to the Springfield rifle' by the end of August 1898. These were being turned out at the rate of 1,300 per day.[60] According to General Breckenridge, bayonets were found to be useless in the Cuban campaign, except to dig with.[61]

Regarding accoutrements, the Ordnance Department supplied the soldier with his cartridge belt, canteen, haversack, knapsack and eating utensils. Also furnished were saddles and harness for the cavalry and artillery. Due to the deterioration of cloth and leather when stored for long periods, the bureau seldom stockpiled these materials in peacetime. Ill-prepared for the huge demand suddenly created in April 1898, Chief of Ordnance General Flagler increased the workforce at the Rock Island Arsenal to 3,000, and installed additional machinery. By mid-August 1898, this plant was turning out 6,000 sets of infantry, cavalry, and artillery accoutrements per day. Flagler also ordered thousands of sets of accoutrements from contractors but, with limited experience in the production of Army goods, their

The Model 1895 undress coat with black mohair braid.

Close-up of the standing collar which was secured by hooks and eyes, and the fly front fastened by six concealed 'gutta-percha' buttons. Photo by the author/ courtesy of Kurt Hughes.

deliveries fell behind schedule, whilst many finished articles were of poor quality.

The U.S. soldier of 1898 wore a woven cartridge waist belt with loops to contain individual rounds. This type of belt had been invented by Captain Anson Mills, 10th U.S. Cavalry, a highly respected career Army officer who was breveted for distinguished conduct in battle. His basic design for a 50-loop leather belt, to replace the Civil War-style cartridge box for campaign use, was first patented on 20 August 1867, and was described as a belt with 'light cylindrical receptacles for cartridges'. Contact between copper cartridges and these leather belts caused a verdigris problem, and encouraged Mills to develop an all-cloth belt. Hence, a second patent, issued to Mills on 31 July 1877, established the woven belt and described the method of 'weaving the body of the belt and its thimbles or pockets in one piece, simultaneously, in one and the same loom...'[62] Mills purchased his first loom in Worcester, Massachusetts, in 1879 and began the production of a belt with integrally-woven cartridge loops. Recommended for adoption by the Army Equipment Board during the same year, 40,000 belts were ordered over a five year period. In order to

meet this demand, Mills entered into a contract with the Gilbert Loom Company of Worcester, Massachusetts, for which he would receive a small royalty. His new belt was first issued to the U.S. Army in 1880. With the completion of this work in 1885, Mills entered into a new contract with his brother-in-law, T.C. Orndorff, who became plant manager of a much-expanded belt manufactory based on ten looms purchased from Gilbert. The Mills & Orndorff relationship lasted until 1901, when the latter's health failed. Anson Mills finally sold the business in 1905, and severed all links with the firm which continued to bear his name.[63]

Being protected by a series of patents, the belts produced by Mills & Orndorff had little or no competition during the life of the woven belt prior to the Spanish-American War, and remained the only model in U.S. service to be constructed in one piece. Made of dark blue cotton webbing which was strong, inexpensive and light-weight, variations of this belt were worn by the Regular Army until the advent of the pocket-type belt after the turn of the century.

Top.
Khaki trousers of the type issued in 1898–1902. This example
has ties at the bottom of the tapered legs.

Middle.
Note the belt loops as well as flat metal buttons for suspenders and four-button fly. The buttons are inscribed 'U.S. ARMY'.

Bottom.
Note the adjustable rear strap and two back pockets. Photos
by the author/courtesy of Kurt Hughes.

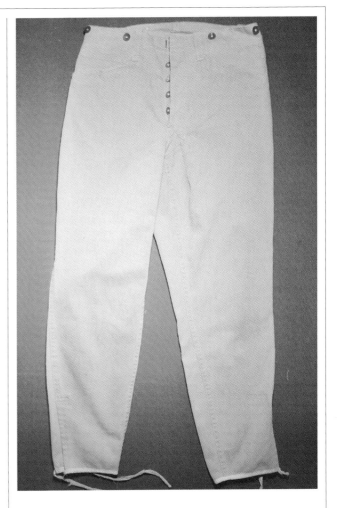

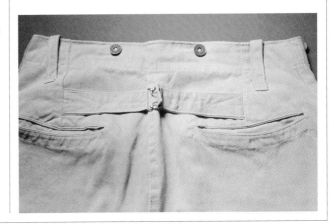

The adoption of the Krag magazine rifle by the U.S. Army in 1892 necessitated a change of loop size on the Mills belt to accommodate the smaller cal. 30 cartridge. The manufacture of belts with a double loop allowing the wearer to carry 100 rounds in 50 double loops was begun around the same time, having been patented on 31 October 1893.

During 1894, a very simple and effective belt fastener, subsequently known as the 'C' hook, was patented. This device consisted of a brass rod passing through the fold of a belt end. The ends of these rods were bent back towards each other, leaving a third of the distance between them left open in the middle. The fold of the other belt end was pinched together, slipping the folded edges into the open gap and on to the rod ends. Thus the two belt ends were held together by a single bent brass rod. Brass keepers could also be slid against the folded ends in order to prevent the belt from loosening.

Measuring 51¾ inches, including brass belt tips, and three inches wide, 300,000 belts of this model were ordered from the Mills-Orndorff company by the U.S. Ordnance Department in April 1898.[64] Although two-thirds of this order had been delivered, and the remainder almost completed, by the end of the 90-day war, the Ordnance Department successfully found alternative sources of belts with which to equip the milling masses of recruits and volunteers assembling in Florida. Foremost among these suppliers were Hurlburt, Spaulding, and Gilbert Loom, none of whom were capable of producing loops as an integral part of the belt. That produced by Hurlbert was 50 inches in length including brass tips, and was made from tan webbing with three woven-in dark blue stripes in both body and loops. Fastened by a wire 'C' closure, this belt carried 100 .30 calibre rounds in loops which were sewn to the belt backing.

Most of the state volunteer regiments received into U.S. service in 1898 were supplied with later versions of the Mills Model 1887 Cartridge Belt fastened by what was commonly known as an 'H' plate, by virtue of its rough similarity to that capital letter. Measuring 47⅜ inches, including the brass tips, this three inch-wide dark blue woven belt carried 45 loops to accommodate the calibre .45 rounds fired by the Springfield rifle. Evidence suggests that some volunteer units were issued with obsolete 'black leather equipments of every description'. Indeed, on 2 August 1898, General Miles telegraphed Secretary of War Alger that such accoutrements, as with the Springfield rifle, be discontinued.[65]

The canteen carried during the conflict in the Caribbean and the Philippines was known as the oblate spheroid tin canteen, and measured 7¾ inches in diameter by three inches thick at its widest point. Until 1898, the only U.S. Army canteens in use were those left over after the Civil War. Modified in 1878, the infantry version was suspended from a one inch-wide dark leather shoulder sling by strong brass hooks secured through triangular wire loops soldered on either side of the canteen rim. The cavalry carried theirs on a shorter dark leather sling with a single heavy snap hook for attachment to either a ring on the saddle, or to a loop on the cartridge belt. All were covered with a felt or wool inner cover and a drab duck outer one which by 1898 invariably bore a black stencilled unit designation. A cork stopper was capped with tin, and attached to the body of the canteen by a three inch-long brass chain passing through a wire ring on top of the stopper. The large number of volunteers required to execute the war against Spain in 1898 necessitated the production of vast numbers of new canteens, which were in turn based on the specifications in use since 1878.[66]

The drab canvas blanket bag was first issued to the U.S. Army in 1878, and was still standard issue supplied to both Regulars, and many Volunteers, during the Spanish-American War. Once in the field, however, many preferred to use 'the horse-collar blanket roll', which contained half a 'shelter tent'. Private Post, of the 71st New York, recalled: 'In the business of making a blanket roll, you lay the blanket on the ground, put into it your tent pegs and your half of the two tent poles – for each man carries but one half of the two tent poles – and then arrange your towel, socks, shirt, and extra underwear and roll up the blanket. Then turning your attention to your half of the tent, fold it lengthwise. This you lay on top of the blanket roll, fasten it at the ends and the middle, much as if reefing a sail, then bend it until it takes its horse-collar shape, fasten the two ends – and there you are, ready to stick your head through and sling it. It is excellent. But – and this we learned on our first march to the transport – the blanket roll must be made

sloppy, not neat. A hard, neat horse collar will bear into the shoulder like a steel bar; so roll it loose and floppy for the part that lies over the shoulder and with no baggage inside the center section – just at the two ends. It looks like a clumsy, amateur sausage lying out straight, but it is soft on the shoulder. In Cuba our horse collars made us look like a bunch of hobo blanket-stiffs; hobos know this trick too – if they can get a blanket.'[67]

Slow deliveries of mess kits caused bitter complaint in the camps. However, by mid-August, the Quartermaster and Ordnance departments had either manufactured or procured, and issued, enough material to provide every soldier with a rifle, a full set of equipage and mess kit, plus a full set of clothing and tentage.

Regarding artillery, the U.S. Army had exchanged the Civil War muzzle-loading cannon for a new arsenal of breech-loading steel guns ranging in calibre from a 3.2-inch light field gun to a 5-inch siege cannon and a 7-inch howitzer. Some state artillery organisations were in receipt of these new models. The Fifth Corps left for Cuba with 16 light field guns, eight large-calibre siege pieces, eight field mortars, four Gatling guns, one Hotchkiss revolving cannon and one experimental dynamite gun. This was supplemented by still more artillery when reinforcements arrived after San Juan and El Caney. The Puerto Rico campaign accumulated 106 guns and mortars of various calibres, plus 10 Gatling guns. The Eighth Corps arrived at Manila with 16 light field guns, six small mountain guns and an assortment of Gatlings and other rapid-fire weapons.

U.S. Regular Army – General Officers and Staff, Full dress

The full dress coat worn by general officers and staff officers at the outbreak of war with Spain had been adopted by the U.S. Army in 1872, and consisted of a double-breasted dark blue frock coat, with a skirt which extended to mid-thigh length. A general had two rows of 12 buttons on the breast which were placed by fours, the distance between each row being 5½ inches at the top and 3½ inches at bottom. The dark blue velvet stand-up collar was between one and two inches in height with rounded corners, and was hooked together at the bottom and thence sloped up and backward at an angle of 30 degrees. The dark blue velvet cuffs were three inches deep with three small buttons at the under seam. There were pockets in the folds of the skirts, with two buttons at the hip and one at the lower end of each pocket, making four buttons

This unidentified infantryman was photographed in 'Ybor City, Fla., by Burgert'. His possible Regular infantry status is indicated by the 'C' clip fastener on his ammunition belt. Anthony Gero Collection.

An unidentified infantryman wearing a khaki field uniform. Note his blouse is faced with 'light sky-blue' on collar, cuffs, shoulder straps and, unofficially, on the pocket flaps. He also wears the original cotton drill belt supplied with this uniform. The unofficial 'crossed rifles' insignia on his hat has an 'E' in the lower angle, and what is probably an '8' in the upper angle. Hence, he possibly belonged to Company E, 8th U.S. Volunteer Infantry. This regiment served as part of the army of occupation in Cuba from 17 August 1898 until 30 March 1899, on which date it sailed back to Savannah, Georgia. An inscription on the back of the photo indicates that this might be Private W. Seifert, who was photographed at the studio of 'R. Tesfar, San Rafael 34, Habana'. Anthony Gero Collection.

on the back and skirt of the coat. The lining was black.

The frock coat worn by a lieutenant general was distinguished by two rows of ten buttons, the upper and lower groups arranged by threes, and the middle groups by fours. A major general wore two rows of nine buttons placed by threes, whilst a brigadier general had two rows of eight buttons placed by pairs. Buttons worn by all general officers and officers of the general staff were gilt and convex, and displayed a spread eagle and stars surrounded by a plain border.

Full dress rank for general officers and staff officers was further indicated by a series of detachable gold epaulettes with solid crescent and 'dead and bright' gold bullion fringe. These were secured by a patent fastener, in use since the 1830s, consisting of an open brass strap on the underside of the epaulette which passed through a cloth loop on the shoulder of the coat and a stud and fastener located at the neck end of the strap. Epaulettes worn by the General of the Army displayed on the strap two 1½ inch diameter, silver embroidered stars with five rays each. In between the

stars was the 'Arms of the United States' embroidered in gold. A lieutenant general wore three stars of the same pattern and colour, ranging in size from 1½, 1¼, 1⅛ inches in diameter; the largest in the centre of the crescent, and the others set longitudinally on the strap, ranging in order of size from the crescent. A major general wore the same, omitting the smallest star, with the smaller of the two remaining stars set in the centre of the strap. A brigadier general wore only the largest star. The Adjutant General, Inspector General and Chief of Record and Pension Office wore an aiguillette, consisting of two breast plaits of ¼ inch

The U.S. Marine attack on the Spanish blockhouse at Cuzco Well, 14 June 1898.

On 10 June 1898, the First Marine Battalion commanded by Colonel R.W. Huntington landed at Guantanamo Bay, Cuba, in order to secure a coaling station and supply base for the U.S. Fleet then blockading Santiago Harbour. The expedition consisted of 21 Marine officers and 615 enlisted men, plus two Navy officers and two seamen. After establishing a beachhead and holding out against persistent Spanish sniper fire and several night time attacks, Huntington decided to crush Spanish resistance in the area. Both the Americans and their enemies were hampered by a shortage of water, but the Spanish, who lacked shipboard distilling equipment, were almost entirely dependent upon a well at the village of Cuzco. Hence, on 14 June, two companies of Marines, accompanied by about 60 Cuban revolutionary reinforcements, attacked a garrison of six companies of Spanish regulars, plus some Cuban loyalists, defending the well at Cuzco. Confronted by

fire from a Spanish blockhouse and a line of trenches concealed in deep bush, Huntington signalled for support fire from the U.S. gunboat *Dolphin* steaming along the shore. In the face of a crossfire, the Spanish retreated having sustained 40 killed, and one officer and 18 men captured. Such was the first fight between Americans and Spanish on Cuban soil.

The painting depicts the moment when the Marines rushed the Spanish positions. They wear the undress summer uniform, and are equipped with the M1895 Navy-issue dark blue woven cartridge belt with black leather pouch flaps. Arms consist of the 6mm Lee straight pull rifle adopted by the Corps in 1895.

The Spanish defenders wear *rayadillo* campaign uniforms, while their officer has donned his full dress *Leopoldina* cap, complete with national cockade. Having served as a sniper until forced back by the American attack, the enlisted man at bottom right still has evidence of fronds of fern and palm leaves fastened in his hat and accoutrement belt. Painting by Richard Hook.

gold-wire cord, and two arm plaits of ³/₁₆ inch cord, attached to the right epaulette.

Epaulettes worn by the Quartermaster General were distinguished by a single star, and a gold, platinum and enamel sword and key, crossed on a wheel, and surmounted by a spread eagle looking to the front. The Paymaster General wore a silver embroidered diamond midway between the star and fastening of the epaulette. The Surgeon General displayed a modification of the cross of Saint John in silver embroidery in the same fashion. The Chief of the Record and Pension Office, a silver embroidered trefoil set within, and partially on, a gold wreath.

Since 1881, all officers with the rank of colonel and below had been permitted to wear shoulder knots and pads, in place of epaulettes. The 'Russian pattern' knot was formed from ¼-inch diameter gold cord at the end of which was a pad covered with a dark blue cloth ground. These were attached to the shoulder by the same device as used with epaulettes. Some staff officers and adjutants also had an aiguillette attached to the right shoulder knot.

Staff officers were distinguished by the following ornamentation, either on the centre of the pad, or midway on the knot, dependent on rank – Adjutant General's Department, a solid silver shield; Inspector General's Department, a solid gold or gilt sword and fasces crossed and wreathed; Judge Advocate's Department, a silver embroidered sword and pen,

Lace-up brown canvas leggings of the type issued to U.S. infantry from 1890. Note the leather straps which buckled up under the shoe. Photo by the author/ courtesy of Kurt Hughes.

crossed and wreathed; Quartermaster's Department, a gold or gilt metal, platinum and enamel sword and key, crossed on a wheel, surmounted by a spread eagle; Subsistence Department, a silver crescent; Medical Department, a modification of the St. John's cross, in silver; Pay Department, a diamond measuring ¾ by one inch placed with shorter diagonal vertical to the

The U.S. infantrymen onboard this troopship display a great variety of early war field dress. The three men seated at centre wear M1895 undress caps and M1883 sack coats. The two at front, and at least three of the men standing behind, have sterling silver marksmen's buttons adorning their collar lapels. The man behind the bugle may well be a musician, as an unofficial 'bugle' patch may just be seen sewn above the elbow on both sleeves of his coat. The soldier standing second from the right wears the enlisted men's sky-blue overcoat with cape thrown back to reveal its dark blue lining. Other overcoats may be seen draped over the stack of weapons and accoutrements. Note the dark blue corporal's chevrons on the cuff of the overcoat on the left. From 'Photographic History of the Spanish American War' (1898).

Opposite.
An unidentified private and corporal of Co. G, 36th U.S. Infantry, wearing khaki blouses of different patterns. The man at left has a blouse conforming precisely to Specification No. 467, dated 9 June 1899, with falling collar; four patch pockets – the upper ones being plaited; and plain, pointed cuffs. Also note his shoulder straps are detachable, a development which occurred after General Orders No. 112, issued on 6 August 1898. The blouse worn by the man at right closely resembles the 'frock' issued to the British Army on foreign service in 1896. Note the low standing collar, permanent shoulder straps, lack of lower pockets, seams either side of the buttoned front, and darts below the pockets. It also appears to have belt loops sewn either side at the waist. US Army Military History Institute/ photo by Jim Enos.

line of the shoulder; Engineer Corps, a silver turreted castle; Ordnance Department, a silver embroidered shell and flame; Signal Corps, two crossed signal flags and a burning torch in gold and silver embroidery; Record and Pension Office, a silver trefoil within and partly upon a gold wreath.

For full dress headgear, all general officers and staff were prescribed a chapeau, or cocked hat, worn with the front peak turned slightly to the left, showing the gilt ornament on the right side. A general officer wore three black ostrich feathers in his hat, while others wore two black ostrich feathers. Trousers worn by all general and staff officers were dark blue, without seam stripe, welt, or cord.

All general officers wore a sash of buff silk net, or buff silk and gold thread, with silk bullion fringe ends, which went twice around the waist and tied behind the left hip. Those above the rank of brigadier general were permitted, at their option, to wear their sash across the body from the left shoulder to the right side.

A water colour by Harry Ogden showing U.S. Army officers in khaki field uniforms. The white shoulder straps worn by the two infantry officers indicate that the artist based the uniforms on those prescribed after the issue of General Orders No. 168, dated 14 September 1899. The mounted officer in the sun helmet depicts General Henry W. Lawton, who commanded the Second Division, Fifth Army Corps, in Cuba in 1898. Peter Newark's Military Pictures.

Swords could be straight or sabre-pattern in brass or steel scabbard. Dress swords of 'appropriate pattern' were permitted for special occasions. Sword knots consisted of a gold cord with acorn end. All officers' sword belts were between 1½ and two inches in width and were worn outside the coat. They were fastened by a gilt rectangular plate, first adopted for all ranks in 1851, which was two inches wide, with a raised bright rim, set within which was a silver laurel wreath encircling the 'Arms of the United States'. Belts of General Officers were of red Russia leather, with three stripes of gold embroidery. Those for Officers of the General Staff and Staff Corps below the rank of field officers had four stripes of gold lace, interwoven with black silk, and lined with black enamelled leather.

A dark blue officer's overcoat, or 'ulster', decorated with four black mohair netted frog buttons, was introduced in 1884. With two side pockets and flaps just below the hips, it extended down the leg from six to eight inches below the knee, and had for general officers a detachable cape of the same colour cloth which reached to the cuffs of the overcoat. This had a three inch wide removable falling collar of black velvet. Rank insignia was indicated on both sleeves by a knot of flat black mohair soutache braid, about ⅛

Below.
The Model 1895 undress cap with 'crossed rifles' insignia and regimental number in the upper angle. The company letter is missing from the lower angle.

Right.
The absence of side vent holes indicates that the maker, George H. Henderson & Co., was not following Quartermaster Department specifications, possibly to save money.

Bottom right.
Interior showing the 'cornucopia' trademark of 'Henderson & Co.' who were situated at the north east corner of 112th and Race streets in Philadelphia. Photos by the author/ courtesy of Kurt Hughes.

inch in width. That for a general officer was composed of five braids in an 'Austrian' knot. The sword belt was worn under the overcoat, with the sword or sabre outside, and the rear sling passing through slits which were added in 1885.

A dark blue cape 'reaching to the tips of the fingers when the arm is extended', with black velvet collar, and black cord fastening, could be worn by all officers 'when not on duty with troops under arms'. This was lined with dark blue for general officers.

General Officers and Staff, Undress

As from 1892, all officers had worn for undress and

The colour party of the 14th U.S. Infantry at Manila in 1901. Each infantry regiment carried a national flag (left), and a blue regimental flag (right). Two men wear still wear the blouse with standing collar and facings on shoulder strap only, authorised on 6 August 1898, while the other two have acquired the blouse with falling collar, prescribed after 9 June 1899. Note the 'C' above the chevrons worn by the colour sergeant holding the national flag. Ben K. Weed Collection.

barracks duty a single-breasted, dark blue sack coat. Based on the service coat worn by the U.S. Navy since 1878, it was trimmed on the collar, and edged around the front, bottom, and side vents at each hip, with lustrous, 1¼ inch-wide, black mohair braid. The original pattern also included black frogging across the chest, and black mohair braid along the two back seams, but this was ordered to be removed via the 1895 regulations. The standing collar was secured by hooks and eyes, and the coat had a fly front fastened by six concealed buttons.

The letters 'U.S.' in gothic capitals of gilt metal, or embroidered in gold, were secured either side of the collar ('U.S.V.' for general officers of Volunteer forces), and were accompanied by the same distinctive departmental insignia as was used on the shoulder knots and pads.

This coat was always worn with shoulder straps measuring 1⅜ inches wide by 4 inches long, of dark blue cloth for general officers and officers of the general staff, corps and departments, bordered with ¼ inch wide gold embroidery. The General of the Army was distinguished by two 5-pointed silver stars, set between which was the gold embroidered 'Arms of the United States'. A lieutenant general wore three silver embroidered stars of the same pattern and size variation as displayed on the epaulette strap for the same rank. A major general bore two silver stars, whilst a brigadier general had one star in the centre of the strap.

A white coat of the same pattern, made of duck or flannel, but without collar insignia or shoulder straps, was worn in hot climates. In 1901, shoulder tabs were added to this garment, which permitted the use of detachable, metal rank and corps insignia, exactly as was worn on the khaki field uniform.

A plain leather belt was worn under the undress coat, and the sword was suspended from the belt hook which protruded through an opening on the left hip. If this coat was worn on field service, or when a pistol was carried, the belt would be worn outside the coat.

The undress cap introduced in 1895 was completely different from any headgear the U.S. Army had worn to date. Replacing the chasseur-pattern forage cap which had been regulation since 1872, it was made of dark blue cloth, and measured 3¼ inches in height all around, with the diameter at the top slightly less than at the base. The band was 1½ inch-wide with ⅛ inch-wide dark blue welts projecting at the top and bottom. The bottom welt was ⅛ inch above the base of the cap. The sloping molded visor was covered and bound with black patent leather, with green felt on the underside. The body of this cap was rigidly stiffened all around from the base to within one inch of the top, the remainder being supported by hair-cloth stiffening. For ventilation, four black eyelets, two on each side, were set above the band. Caps worn by general officers had a cord of ¼-inch diameter gold bullion secured at both ends by small eagle buttons, and were embellished with a band of black velvet which filled the space between the welts. All other staff officers wore a band of black mohair. The cap badge for all officers was the U.S. coat of arms embroidered in gold. A black oilcoth cover could be fitted over this cap in wet weather. A white cotton cap of the same pattern was prescribed for tropical climates. Undress trousers for general officers and staff were the same as worn with full dress. Plain white duck or flannel trousers were worn in hot climates.

General Officers and Staff, Field dress

Shortly after the outbreak of war with Spain, the Adjutant General's Office approved two new blouses for 'field dress' use by officers. Possibly based on a design suggested by Captain Theo Bingham, who did much to promote the idea that the U.S. Army needed a more servicable uniform for campaign purposes, both of these garments were presumably felt to be more practical than the smart 1895 undress coat, with its stand-up collar and generous trim.[68] On 7 May 1898, General Orders No. 38 authorised a dark blue cloth, or serge, blouse. To facilitate 'field service', this

Company B of the 3rd U.S. Artillery was photographed at Fort Monroe, Virginia, during 1898. They were the only unit of their regiment to be stationed on the East Coast at the beginning of the war, the rest being either on the West Coast, in Oregon, or Florida. They wear M1883 sack coats and M1895 undress caps with 'crossed cannon' insignia. Note the chevrons and trouser seam stripes on the two N.C.O.s seated in the front row. The bugler has two half inch-wide musician's welts on his trousers, whilst the N.C.O. holding the kitten has a Heavy Artillery First Class Gunner's badge on his left breast. Several men are wearing regulation 'C-clip' Mills belts which emphasise their role as heavy artillerymen. Frank Barrowcliff Coll., USAMHI/photo by Jim Enos.

garment had four outside pockets with flaps buttoned down with small regulation 'eagle' gilt buttons. The two breast pockets had a two-inch wide box plait in the centre. The collar was 'rolled', or stand-and-fall, and the skirt was designed to extend between one third and one half the distance between the hip and knee. For generals and officers of the general staff this garment was double-breasted with large regulation gilt buttons arranged in the same manner, according to rank, as was worn on the frock coat. Collar insignia was the same as that worn for undress, as were the shoulder straps. Trousers worn with this blouse were the same as prescribed for undress.[69]

Officers' blue 'Serge Blouses' were available from 'The Pettibone Bro. Mfg. Co., Military Purveyors', of Cincinnati, Ohio, by 21 May, and from 'Oehm & Co., Army and Navy Outfitters' of Baltimore, Maryland, by 18 June. Both companies advertised them as being 'full skeleton or half lined' in order to contend with the tropical heat of Cuba and the Philippines.[70]

On 9 May 1898, General Orders No. 39 approved a blouse of similar pattern for 'all Commissioned Officers', with matching trousers or breeches (for mounted officers), but made of 'cotton drilling or khakie [sic], light brown color...'[71] With a low straight-standing collar and pointed sleeve cuffs, this garment was fastened by only a single row of five large regulation gilt buttons and, as with the dark blue blouse, had four outside pockets with flaps. A single,

Below.
A M1899 cork 'Summer Helmet', covered with fine drab drill cloth, and modelled roughly on the British pattern of the period.

Bottom left.
Note the long rear brim.

Left.
Interior showing cork body and green cotton twill lining. Photos by the author/courtesy of Kurt Hughes.

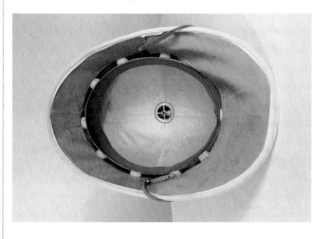

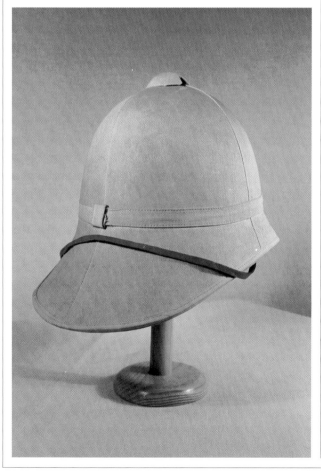

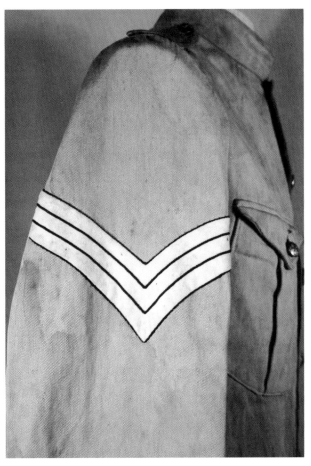

Above.

This khaki infantry sergeant's blouse, complete with full infantry accoutrements, was issued sometime after 6 August 1898, when General Orders No. 112 required that facing colours be removed from all but the shoulder straps.

Above right.

The same blouse showing the two inch-wide, box plait extended down the middle of the back. The loops which supported the cotton drill belt orginally supplied with this uniform may just be seen underneath the Mills belt.

Right.

1899 Regulations stated that chevrons on the khaki blouse could be 'of such material as may be found most suitable for service.' This sergeant possibly removed the white cotton chevrons from his dark blue wool flannel sack coat and attached them to his field dress. Hence the mixture of facing colours. Photo by the author/ courtesy of Kurt Hughes.

The Hospital Corpsmen boarding this train display similar rank and specialist insignia to that prescribed for the Regular Army. However, they appear to be volunteers as the Hospital Stewards wear red crosses set within white, as opposed to green, chevrons on their coat sleeves, while privates are distinguished by a single small white patch on each arm bearing the red cross. The infantry sergeant major from North Carolina in full marching appears to be carrying a Merriam pack. From 'Photographic History of the Spanish-American War' (1898).

two inch-wide, box plait extended down the middle of the back from the collar to the bottom of the skirt. Attached to each shoulder was a strap which reached from the sleeve seam, where it was 1½ inches wide, to about half an inch from the collar seam, where it narrowed to one inch in width. This was fastened at the latter point by a small regulation gilt button. In line with the facing colours prescribed for the M1884 full dress frock coat, General Orders No. 39 stipulated that the 'cuffs, [shoulder] straps and collar' of the new khaki blouse were to be 'of the same material as the coat and of the color of the facings of the arm'.[72] This was subsequently clarified in General Order No. 51, dated 23 May, which listed the facing colours for various arms of service – in the case of general officers

and officers of the general staff, corps, and departments, this was to be 'dark sky blue (color of the trousers of the officers of the line)'. This is a probable reference to the dark blue trousers prescribed for general officers, and officers of the general staff.[73] These coloured facings were usually added to the pocket flaps as well, although no official orders have been found which authorised this.

All insignia of rank and corps worn on the khaki blouse were of the same pattern as that prescribed for undress shoulder straps, but were metal and detachable. Officers of the rank of colonel and above displayed their rank insignia on the cloth shoulder straps, whilst the U.S. coat of arms, accompanied by the appropriate corps badge, was worn either side of the collar. Although the letters 'U.S.', or 'U.S.V.', where applicable, were not orginally permitted to be worn on this blouse, officers of Volunteers did indeed wear such letters on their collar, as photographs of the period indicate.

The khaki trousers authorised at this time differed in cut from the old straight-legged, or 'stove-pipe', sky-blue kersey type, being designed to fit loose above the knee and tapered to 'follow the shape of the leg from above the calf to the top of the shoe'. The latter feature was incorporated to accommodate the use of leggings. Whilst retaining the adjustable strap at the rear, they did away with the time-honoured U.S. military dependence on suspenders for support by incorporating four belt loops. Mounted officers received breeches of the same colour and cloth, which fitted 'close at knee and below', to be worn with either shoes and leggings or boots.[74] Both patterns were devoid of seam stripes, and deviated from a U.S. military practice that dated to at least the 1830s. Alternatively, officers could wear trousers 'of [blue] cloth of the usual colors and facings', but cut in the same style as the new khaki ones.

Field dress headgear for general officers consisted of the Model 1889 black or drab felt hat, with a gold cord. Another break with the past was the choice of 'fair or russet leather shoes or boots', in lieu of the traditional black foot-wear, to be worn with the khaki field uniform.

Military outfitters of the day were quick to respond to the demand for the new khaki uniform. By 4 June

1898, 'Brooks Brothers' of New York advertised in the *Army and Navy Journal* that they were 'prepared to make [the] uniform blouse and breeches from the genuine imported "Khaki," in the shade and weight adopted by the War Department...'[75] In the same journal, 'Pettibone Brothers' of Cincinnati announced: 'The new Khakie *[sic]* Uniform for Officers is now ready.'[76] Two weeks later, other firms had joined in the sales campaign, despite obvious spelling difficulties. 'A. Schuman & Co.' of Boston advertised 'High Grade Officers' Uniforms, to measure, made from Genuine English Kharkee Fabric.' New York-based 'Luckey & Sammis, Army and Navy Tailors' offered for sale 'Kahrkee (Correct Spelling) *[sic]* Army Officers Uniforms.' In Philadelphia, 'Jacob Reed's Sons' more accurately promoted a full range of 'Genuine Imported Khaki Cloth Field Service Uniforms... Extra Light Weight, $12.00, Light Weight, 13.50, Medium Weight, 14.50, Special Fine Quality, 18.00.'[77]

Some officers clearly acquired the new field dress very quickly. When the staff of Major General Miles inspected the camps of the Regulars at Tampa on 6 June, an *Army and Navy Journal* correspondent commented: 'The new uniforms worn by Maj. Seyburn, Capt. Alger and others... are cool looking, comfortable and durable. 'Tis a pity the whole Army cannot have the uniform before leaving; the heavy

The buglers of the 1st Vermont Volunteer Infantry were photographed at Camp Thomas, Chickamauga, in Georgia, on 30 June 1898. The regiment remained in the U.S. as part of the Seventh Army Corps, and was mustered out before the end of the year. Note the Chief Trumpeter standing at centre. Anthony Gero Collection.

This Harry Ogden water colour depicts khaki field uniforms worn by enlisted men. Clearly produced after the issue of General Orders No. 168, the shoulder straps and chevrons worn by the infantry sergeant are white. The artillery first sergeant and the mounted cavalry trooper both wear 'summer helmets', much in use in 1898. Note the Cuban blockhouse in the background. Peter Newark's Military Pictures.

blue... makes one hot by its suggestiveness of being entirely unsuited to these latitudes.'[78]

U.S. Regular Infantry, Full dress

The Colonel, Lieutenant Colonel, and Major of infantry wore a frock coat with two rows of nine gilt, convex buttons bearing a spread eagle having a shield with the letter 'I' on its chest, placed at equal distance on the breast. Collar and cuffs were the same colour and material as the coat. A captain, first lieutenant, second lieutenant and additional second lieutenant wore the same, except that there were only seven buttons in each row.

The standard fatigue wear for the U.S. Army was the Model 1883 dark blue wool flannel blouse, or 'sack coat'. The lining was often removed for sub-tropical service in 1898. Photo by the author/ courtesy of Dusan Farrington.

Rank was indicated by gold shoulder knots and pads of the same pattern as for the staff corps, but on a white cloth base representing the 'arm of service' colour for infantry adopted in 1884.[79] Rank insignia for a colonel consisted of a silver embroidered eagle in the centre of the pad; a lieutenant colonel was distinguished by two silver embroidered leaves, one at each end of the pad; a major by the same, only in gold; a captain, two silver embroidered bars at each end of the pad; a first lieutenant, one silver embroidered bar either end of the pad; second lieutenant and additional second lieutenant, a plain pad.

Full dress headgear, adopted in 1881, consisted of a

Below.
Light artillery full dress helmet with horse hair plume and worsted breast cord. Photo by the author/courtesy of Dusan Farrington.

Bottom right.
Dark sky-blue artillery trousers with NCO's seam stripes or welts. Photo by the author/courtesy of Dusan Farrington.

Regimental flag of the 1st U.S. Artillery, measuring 4' 4" on the staff by 5' 6" on the fly. Since 1888, the field of an artillery regiment had been scarlet silk with a yellow fringe, bearing in the centre two crossed cannon, with the letters 'U.S.' above in scarlet on a yellow scroll and, underneath, the number of the regiment in the same style. Ben K. Weed Collection.

helmet with a cork body covered with black cloth or felt. All trimmings, including a cord and tassel attached from the left side of the helmet to the coat and chain chin strap were gilt. Insignia consisted of a gilt plate bearing the eagle, with motto, and shield with the number of the regiment on it in white, behind which were crossed rifles. Helmets worn by field grade officers, as well as the regimental adjutant, were topped with socket and plume of white buffalo or yak hair. Company grade officers were distinguished by a gilt spike. Small brass side buttons bore the crossed rifles insignia of infantry.[80]

Trousers were of the darker 'sky-blue' kersey first introduced in 1885, with adjustable backstrap, buttons on the outside of the waistband for suspenders and 'frog' pockets which opened on the top and at the side, being fastened by a single button in the top outside corner. Infantry officers were distinguished by a 1½ inch wide white welt on the outside seams. Plain white duck or flannel trousers were worn during the summer months.

Until 1902, infantry officers were required to carry the 1860 pattern staff and field officer's sword, attached to a black enamelled belt embellished with one broad stripe of gold lace. Company grade officers' belts were decorated with four gold lace stripes, interwoven with white silk, and lined with black enameled leather. The full dress sword knot for all officers consisted of a gold lace strap with gold bullion tassel. In the field, all officers wore a sword knot of plaited leather or webbing.

Infantry officers' overcoats were the same basic colour and pattern as that worn by general officers, but had a detachable hood of the same colour as the coat, which was lined with black 'Italian cloth'. Sleeve rank insignia, of the same material as that used for general officers, consisted of a trefoil loop of five braids for a colonel, four for a lieutenant colonel, three for a major, two for a captain and one for a first lieutenant. A second lieutenant had plain sleeves. Infantry officers' capes were officially to be lined with white cloth, although many officers appear to have purchased light blue-lined capes.

As a result of an Order issued by Secretary of War Alger on 3 August 1898, all new army recruits after that date were 'not required to draw full dress uniforms', as during the existing war 'none but field or undress uniforms' were to be worn by the enlisted man in the field.[81] By July 1899, the Quartermaster's Department was considering plans to 'do away with the dress coat for enlisted men'.[82] This was finally implemented in 1902, when a whole new uniform was authorised.

The full dress uniform issued to infantry N.C.O.s and enlisted men prior to that date consisted of the Model 1884 single-breasted, dark blue frock coat fastened by nine buttons, of the same pattern as worn by officers. This was piped down the front edges with white cord, while the standing collar and shoulder tabs were faced with white cloth. The cuffs displayed white patches ornamented with three small buttons. The rear skirts were faced with elongated white patches, decorated with six small buttons, on either side of the opening, which was also piped with white. Worn under this was a white linen collar and black cravat. Shirts for full dress were usually of white muslin.

Chevrons for N.C.O.s were of gold lace for full dress, and were worn point down above the elbow. The bars of the chevrons were ½ inch wide, with black chain stitching on white cloth ground. Rank and specialist insignia was indicated as follows: sergeant major (from 1899, regimental sergeant major) – three bars and an arc of three bars; quartermaster sergeant (from 1899, regimental quartermaster sergeant) – three bars and a tie of three bars; chief musician (adopted 1899) – three bars and an arc of two bars, with a bugle in the centre; principal musician – three bars and a bugle; regimental color sergeant – three bars and a sphere, 1¼ inches in diameter; regimental color sergeant (as revised in 1901) – three bars, with a five-pointed star in the centre; battalion sergeant major (adopted in 1899) – three bars and an arc of two bars; company sergeant major (adopted in 1898) – three bars and a tie of one bar; drum major – three bars and two crossed batons; first sergeant – three bars and a lozenge; company quartermaster sergeant – three bars and a tie of one bar; sergeant – three bars; corporal – two bars; pioneer (discontinued in 1899) – crossed axes; lance corporal (adopted in 1891) – one bar; artificer (adopted in 1899) – crossed hammers; cook – a white cook's cap (adopted in 1898).

The full dress helmet for infantry enlisted men, introduced in 1881, was covered with black cloth and topped with a spike and base of brass. Insignia on the front consisted of brass eagle plate with 'crossed rifles' and the number of the regiment in white metal on the shield. The leather chin strap was secured either end by small regulation 'crossed rifle' buttons. Trousers were sky blue kersey, 'made loose without plaits', and were 'to spread well over' the footwear which, before May of 1898, consisted of bootees or brogans of black leather. Infantry N.C.O.s' trouser welts were white as follows: sergeant – one inch wide; corporal and lance corporal – ½ inch wide; and musicians – two ½ stripes.

All enlisted men were issued a sky-blue cloth, double-breasted overcoat, with detachable cape lined with dark blue. N.C.O.s' chevrons on this garment were of dark blue cloth, attached below the elbow.

U.S. Regular Infantry, Undress

The infantry officers' M1895 undress coat, trimmed with mohair, was the same as that worn by general officers, with collar insignia consisting of the letters 'U.S.' in gothic capitals ('U.S.V.' for officers of Volunteer forces), next to which were two crossed rifles, one inch high, with the number of the regiment above the intersection – all in gold or gilt metal, or embroidered in gold.

Shoulder straps were of the same dimensions as those of general officers, and bore the following insignia embroidered on a white ground: a colonel – silver spread eagle; lieutenant colonel – a silver leaf at either end of the strap; a major – the same, only in gold; captain – two silver bars either end of the strap; first lieutenant – one silver bar either end of the strap; second lieutenant and additional second lieutenant – a plain white strap. As with the general officers and staff, a white duck or flannel coat of the same pattern, but without collar insignia or shoulder straps, was worn in hot climates. Shoulder tabs bearing insignia were added in 1901.

The infantry officers' M1895 undress cap was the same as that worn by general officers and staff, except for the band between the two welts, which was of black mohair braid. Undress trousers were the same as those worn with full dress. N.C.O.s and enlisted men did not have an undress uniform.

U.S. Regular Infantry, Field Uniform

On 7 May 1898, all infantry officers were prescribed a single-breasted version of the dark blue serge blouse, with four outside pockets. Collar insignia and shoulder straps were the same as worn with the undress coat. Headgear could either be the M1895 undress cap, or the M1889 campaign hat with cord of gold and black intermixed.

The khaki blouse prescribed for infantry officers on 9 May was the same pattern and cut as that worn

by general officers and officers of the general staff. Officers below the grade of colonel wore rank insignia on their cloth shoulder straps, 'about one-third distant from the shoulder seam to the collar'. The U.S. coat of arms was affixed midway between this rank insignia and the collar seam. In the field, these rank insignia did not prove popular. After the attack on San Juan Hill, a correspondent of the *Army and Navy Journal* reported many officers, 'seeing that the fire was especially directed against them, tore off their shoulder straps, seized rifles from fallen men, put on cartridge belts and in this disguise led their men'.[83]

As per General Orders 39 and 51 – and breaking with previous regulations for full dress and undress which stipulated white for infantry – the collar, shoulder straps and cuffs for infantry blouses were faced with 'light sky blue (color of the trousers of the enlisted men)', while many examples were unofficially faced on the pocket flaps with the same colour.

The M1889 felt campaign hat worn by infantry officers could be either black or drab, and was often worn without the prescribed gold and black cord. Since 1880, officers had also been permitted to wear in hot climates a cork 'Summer Helmet', covered with fine white wool cloth, and modelled roughly on the British pattern of the period. In 1899, this was superseded by a slightly different helmet covered with khaki drill, with a longer rear brim.

Before the war with Spain, U.S. regular infantry N.C.O.s and enlisted men wore for field dress a Model 1883 dark blue wool flannel blouse, or 'sack coat', fastened by a single row of five large regulation gilt buttons. Three smaller buttons of the same pattern were attached to each cuff. This garment could be made with or without a lining. N.C.O.s' chevrons were the same as worn with full dress, but in white cloth. The 'light sky-blue' kersey trousers prescribed for full dress were also worn with this coat . A shortage of standard sky-blue in May 1898 led to the purchase of dark-blue cloth for trousers, so that the men might be more quickly supplied.[84]

Canvas fatigue clothing, originally adopted in 1884 and consisting of a five-button sack coat and trousers

Cavalry version of the M1895 undress cap with 'crossed sabres' insignia and designation indicating that the wearer belonged to Troop G, 1st U.S. Cavalry. Photo by the author/ courtesy of Dusan Farrington.

This view of Chaplain Henry A. Brown preaching to the 'Rough Riders' shows the light-brown canvas cavalry stable dress acquired by the regiment before their departure for Cuba. Note the one-piece shoulder yoke and centre seam down the back of the coats. General Wheeler, Colonel Wood and Lieutenant Colonel Roosevelt are stood in the distant far right. John Sickles Collection.

of 6-ounce cotton duck dyed brown, was made available on a mass scale at the beginning of the war, and was used until khaki cotton drill could be supplied in sufficient quality and quantity.

Although merely listed with 'chambray shirts' and 'white muslin shirts' as an option in the 1899 regulations, the dark blue wool flannel pullover shirt, which had been worn by the U.S. Army on the Western Frontier since 1875, was utilised on a mass scale during the period 1898–1902. Indeed, Colonel William S. Patten, Assistant Quartermaster at Washington, D.C., stated during May 1899: 'The Department is making an earnest endeavour to educate the troops to use the blue flannel shirt instead of the Chambray or linen shirt, as in a measure it serves the hygienic purpose of the abdominal bandages, and is believed to be a great protection against sickness.'[85] This shirt was produced with

numerous variations in cut and style, dependent on which depot or clothing contractor produced the goods. All had falling collars and three small buttons at the front. Most had two patch pockets on the chest, which were usually fastened by the same type of button. Produced in lighter-weight fabric, this was the most comfortable dress for tropical campaigning, for officers as well as enlisted men. Permission for officers to attach the 'ordinary insignia of rank' to the collars of their dark blue shirts 'in the field during extreme warm weather' was granted via Circular 26 as early as 25 July 1898.[86] This Circular also first authorised N.C.O.s to sew their chevrons to their dark blue shirt-sleeves. On 14 September 1899, General Orders No. 168 reiterated these concessions.[87] Both measures represented an important step which deviated from past regulations and practices. A lighter-weight woollen khaki pullover shirt patterned after the dark blue version was developed in 1900, and was issued to troops in the Philippines during the period 1901–1902.[88]

Headgear at the beginning of the war generally consisted of the Model 1895 undress cap and the drab-coloured felt campaign hat of the pattern introduced in 1889. The cap was the same as that worn by officers, but with an enamelled leather chin strap secured by two regulation buttons, a brass 'crossed rifles' insignia with the number of the regiment in the upper angle, and the letter of the company in the lower angle. White linen caps of the same pattern, minus side vent holes, were available for troops stationed at Fort Monroe, Jackson Barracks, Key West, Washington Barracks, Fort Barrancas and Sullivans Island.

The 1889-pattern campaign hat was required to be worn with an indented crown, either side of which was punched a 'star-shaped' series of ventilation holes. The brim was strengthened with three rows of stitching, but was raw-edged instead of turned over. Although regulations stipulated that this was to be worn with a white worsted hat cord with acorn terminals, over the brown silk band, the former was often ommitted on campaign. The crowns of these hats were frequently re-shaped into a fashionable, but unofficial, 'Montana peak'. During June 1899, the Philadelphia depot produced an experimental batch of 1,000 hats with brass screen ventilators on each side of the crown, to a larger size than those fitted to hats prior to 1889. After July 1899, brass metal insignia in the form of a regimental number over company letter was authorised to be worn on the front of the campaign hat. Unofficially, many infantrymen appear to have removed the 'crossed rifles' insignia from their M1895 undress cap and fastened them on either the front or side of the crown of their campaign hats.

During the late 1880s, the U.S. military began to see the wisdom of providing leggings as part of the campaign uniform. Made of 15-ounce brown cotton duck reinforced with strips of tanned horsehide, and usually fastened by a system of laces and hooks, they were designed to protect the trousers from under the knee to the ankle. The first leggings, which appear to have been a 'chocolate' brown colour, were officially introduced for all branches of service in 1890 but were not included in the dress regulations until 1899. Those issued to infantry were made from 15 ounce brown canvas, and were 12 inches high with lace fastenings running through seven grommets and six hooks. William H. Wiley, of Hartford, Connecticut, claimed to have made 'all the leggins of the U.S. Army and all branches of the Government service for eleven years' on 4 June 1898. Advertised in *Army and Navy Journal*, his 'Regulation Infantry Leggins' were 65 cents per pair.[89]

Although the khaki uniform adopted on 9 May 1898 was officially intended for officers only, it quickly became apparent that enlisted men would eventually receive uniforms of the same colour. On 23 April 1898, the *Army and Navy Journal* announced : 'The uniforms of officers and men will be exactly alike except for the insignia of rank on the collar and shoulders... The new uniforms resemble the Kaliki [sic] uniforms used in East Indian campaigns. They are of drab canvas, light in weight and admirably adapted for wear in tropical climates.'[90]

The first official evidence that enlisted men were to have uniforms made from a lightweight yellowish-brown canvas twill or duck is included in General Orders No. 51, dated 23 May 1898, which stipulated that the facings of the coat for both officers *and men* were to be coloured according to the traditional pattern, but with the infantry wearing 'light sky-blue'. The Second Edition of the *Regulations and Decisions Pertaining to the Uniform of the United States Army*, published on 20 June 1898, went on to refer in a footnote to field uniforms for enlisted men 'being manufactured under special authority'.[91]

Evidence suggests that a number of slightly different styles of blouse were produced by various contractors, who all based their work on an 'extended pattern' using General Orders No. 39 and the old undress five-button sack coat as a model. As with officers' blouses, many of those made for enlisted men had unofficial facings of 'light sky-blue' on the pocket flaps as well as on the collar, shoulder straps and cuffs. Most versions had box plaits in the breast pockets and plain hip pockets. Pocket flaps varied from deep to shallow to almost rectangular. Collars varied from straight standing to standing-falling, to rolled down, as on the blue sack coat. Sleeve cuffs were mostly pointed, although some were plain. Shoulder straps on most seem to have been sewn on permanently, although examples survive with detachable straps, or none at all. Matching belts made from the same fabric as the blouse, secured by buttons at the front, and supported by loops at the back, were also a distinctive feature on many garments. N.C.O.s' chevrons were the same as for full dress, but of 'light sky-blue'.

Some men were photographed wearing blouses with no lower pockets. This blouse-type bears a remarkable resemblance to the British khaki foreign service jacket universally adopted in 1896, which saw extensive Boer War service, and raises the tantalising possibility that some British-made uniforms were worn by U.S. troops during the conflict in Cuba and the Philippines. Certainly, English khaki cloth was readily available to military outfitters early in the war, and appears to have been worn on a widespread basis by American officers, as already indicated. During 1899, the Chief Quartermaster in Manila, J.W. Pope, purchased for enlisted men about 100,000 suits of khaki, 'the material furnished from Manchester,

Top left.

This cavalry corporal's khaki blouse was issued after 9 June 1899, on which date Specification No. 467 called for a falling collar and plain seam down the centre of the back, in place of a box plait. Note also that the yellow cavalry facings are found on the shoulder straps only, as per General Orders No. 112, dated 6 August 1898.

Above.

The plaited breast pockets appear to have been set higher by this time, the top of the pocket being level with the second front button.

Left.

Note that permanent shoulder straps were still in use at this time. Photos by the author/ courtesy of Dusan Farrington.

England'. This cloth may have been supplied by E. Spinner & Co., of Manchester and Bombay, who advertised 'Patent Fast Dyed Khaki Materials – Universally worn by the British Troops in India, Egypt, etc.' in the *Army and Navy Journal* towards the end of 1898.[92]

A number of further modifications were made to the khaki blouse for both officers and men between 1898 and 1902. Circular 25, issued by the Adjutant General's Office on 20 July 1898, authorised the wearing of metal insignia on the collar – in the case of infantry, 'crossed rifles'.[93] Being concerned that facing

colours proved 'too conspicuous a mark' when fighting a guerrilla enemy in jungle terrain, the Secretary of War approved General Orders No. 112, dated 6 August 1898, which stated that henceforth 'facings, conforming in color to the respective arms of service ['light sky-blue' in the case of infantry], shall be worn by officers and men upon the shoulder straps only.'[94] The cuffs were also re-enforced with a double layer of khaki cloth at this time – presumably to compensate for the lack of facing colour. As a result, contractors were probably ordered to discontinue the manufacture of blouses with full facings, though their issue and wear doubtless carried on until supplies were exhausted. Indeed, it was not until 6 July 1899 that Adjutant General Corbin advised General Otis in Manila that the regulation pattern blouse would in future be without facings, 'except on shoulder straps'.[95] After the issue of General Orders No. 112, shoulder straps were made detachable and interchangeable in an effort to simplify the problem of supply to enlisted men.

During the Fall of 1898, the Quartermaster General finally set a standard for the manufacture of

khaki cotton cloth from a domestic supplier, via Specification No. 455, *Specifications for Khaki Cloth*, dated 11 October. This presumably applied to true khaki cotton, rather than canvas, uniforms but the exact pattern was not specified until 9 June 1899, when Specification No. 467 called for a blouse made from seven and a half to eight ounce fabric, fastened by a single row of five detachable gilt regulation buttons, and a falling collar, plain pointed cuffs, four patch pockets (the upper ones being plaited), and a plain seam down the centre of the back, rather than a box plait.

On 14 September 1899, General Orders No. 168 changed the colour of infantry shoulder straps, the

Right.

The two rows of stitching around the brim of this cavalry campaign hat may indicate it was made sometime prior to 1889. The brass letters on its front indicate it belonged to a member of Company D, 8th Cavalry. Additional pin holes either side suggest the wearer may at one time have unofficially attached a cavalry 'crossed sabres' insignia. The acorn terminals suggest that the hat cord was 1889-issue.

Below.

The 'star-shaped' vent can be clearly seen on the crown.

Photos by the author courtesy of Dusan Farrington.

64 U.S. Forces

sole remaining facings on the khaki blouse, to white.[96] This was presumably designed to fall back in line with the full dress and undress trim colour for officer's transverse shoulder straps, N.C.O.s' chevrons and the trouser seam welt. In order to make mass distribution easier, these shoulder strap facings were also detachable.

U.S. Regular Artillery, Full dress

Artillery officers wore the same pattern of dark blue, full dress frock coat, with the same insignia of rank, as for infantry, but with the following differences. The buttons bore a spread eagle having a shield with the letter 'A' on its chest. The cloth ground of the shoulder knots was scarlet, with the number of the regiment and insignia of rank embroidered in silver. Full dress pattern 1881 helmets bore the gilt crossed cannon insignia and were adorned with a red buffalo-hair plume. Trousers were dark sky-blue with 1½ inch-wide scarlet welts. During the summer months, plain white duck or flannel trousers were permitted.

All artillery officers were authorised to carry the light artillery sabre and scabbard. For full dress, those of field grade wore sword belts of black enamelled leather decorated with one broad stripe of gold lace. Company grade officers' belts had four stripes of gold lace, interwoven with scarlet silk, and lined with black enamelled leather. The overcoat was the same pattern as worn by infantry officers, but the cape was lined with scarlet.

N.C.O.s and enlisted artillerymen wore the same pattern of dark blue frock coat as the infantry, except

Opposite.

Lieutenant Colonel Theodore Roosevelt, 1st U.S. Volunteer Cavalry, wears the regulation Model 1898 khaki field dress with yellow facings on the collar, cloth shoulder straps, and probably the cuffs. The gold-edged yellow shoulder straps worn transversely over the cloth ones are non-regulation on this uniform, as are his brass collar insignia, which consist of the letters 'U.S.V.' and 'crossed sabres' above which is the numeral '1'. The latter insignia is also used to pin back the brim on his drab campaign hat. The famous blue polka-dot handkerchief may just be seen showing above his collar. Peter Newark's American Pictures.

Below.

Troop D, 1st U.S. Volunteer Cavalry, wearing their brown canvas stable dress, and holding Krag carbines. The seventh man from the left in the front rank is William Pollock, son of the Pawnee chief Big Eagle. His blood-curdling war whoops on San Juan Hill were long remembered by both Spanish and American combatants. John Sickles Collection.

The flag carried by the 1st U.S. Volunteer Cavalry at San Juan Hill. Based on the M1887 regular army cavalry flag, it was hand painted by Horstman Brothers of Philadelphia, and measured three feet on the staff by four feet on the fly. Ben K. Weed Collection.

that the facing colour and piping was scarlet. N.C.O.s and enlisted men of light artillery wore an 1888-pattern dress coat fastened with a single row of nine regulation buttons. Introduced via General Orders No. 6, it had shorter skirts with eight-inch slits at the sides. More elaborate scarlet facings on the skirts were ornamented with only four buttons. The coat front, skirt bottoms and side slits were also piped red. The full dress M1881 helmet for foot artillery enlisted men was topped with a spike and base of brass. Insignia on the front consisted of a brass eagle plate with 'crossed cannon' and the number of the regiment in the shield. The leather chin strap was secured either end by small regulation 'crossed cannon' buttons.

N.C.O.s' rank insignia, in gold lace on red cloth ground, was as per infantry with addition of the following – a Mechanic and Artificer wore on his sleeves two crossed hammers, of red cloth; a First-Class Gunner was distinguished in dress coat, blouse and overcoat, by a 1½ inch-long, red cloth, elongated

cannon projectile 'neatly piped and stitched on the outside of the right sleeve halfway between the point of the shoulder and elbow, below the chevrons in case of a noncommissioned officer'; Veterinary Sergeant of Battery of Field Artillery, three bars and a horseshoe, 'worn toe uppermost, above the inner angle of the chevron'. Trousers for light artillerymen were of 'sky-blue' kersey with a reenforced saddle piece, of the same material, on the seat and inside legs. Welts along the seams were the same as for infantry, only in scarlet.

U.S. Regular Artillery, Undress

For undress, the collar insignia on the M1895 dark blue undress coat for artillery officers consisted of two, one inch-high, crossed cannon, of gold or gilt metal, or embroidered in gold, with the number of the regiment at the intersection. Shoulder strap insignia was the same as for infantry, but on a scarlet cloth ground. A plain black leather belt was worn for undress. Undress cap insignia was the U.S. coat of arms, as per infantry officers.

U.S. Regular Artillery, Field Uniform

The dark blue blouse for artillery officers, prescribed

via General Orders No. 38 in May 1898, was the same as that worn by infantry officers, except for the gold or gilt metal collar insignia, which featured two 1 inch high 'crossed cannon' with the number of the regiment in the upper angle and company letter in lower angle.

The artillery version of the khaki uniform

A drab campaign hat of the type worn by all branches of the U.S. Army during war with Spain. With regulation 'fore and aft' indentation, the woollen hat cord has quite typically been removed for campaign duty. Photo by the author/courtesy of Kurt Hughes.

A dark blue Mills cartridge belt with 'H'-shaped plate, of the type issued to U.S. Volunteers in 1898. Photo by the author/courtesy of Dusan Farrington.

prescribed for officers during the same month bore the rank insignia as for infantry officers, and was faced with scarlet on the collar, cuffs, and shoulder straps. As for infantry, it was also unofficially faced with this colour on the pocket flaps, in many cases. This was later reduced to shoulder strap facings only via General Orders No. 112, dated 6 August 1898. Khaki trousers for mounted artillery officers were reinforced in the seat and inside leg.

Armed with the 'Trapdoor' Springfield rifles, this well-equipped Volunteer unit is undergoing kit inspection prior to departure for active service. Note their cartridge belts are fastened by 'H' plates, and their fatigue blouse collars have worsted cord trim around the collar – a feature reminiscent of the Model 1874 sack coats, and still used by some National Guard and state militia. Each man also seems to have broad seam stripes on his trousers – a distinction reserved for officers and NCOs in the Regular Army. From 'Photographic History of the Spanish-American War' (1898).

Prior to the war with Spain, N.C.O.s and enlisted men of the artillery service wore the same M1883 dark blue wool flannel sack coat as per infantry. N.C.O.s' chevrons were the same as worn with full dress, but of red cloth. The 'sky-blue' trousers prescribed for full dress were also worn with this coat. Heavy artillery units manning coastal batteries in the U.S. also served as infantry, and were issued with Krag rifles and accompanying infantry accoutrements.

Enlisted men of artillery units on active service in Cuba and the Philippines at the beginning of the war wore dark blue wool flannel shirts with sky blue trousers, duck leggings and drab campaign hats with red wool hat cord. When eventually supplied, khaki uniforms consisted of the same pattern of blouse as

that issued to infantry, with scarlet facings as per officers. N.C.O.s' chevrons were the same as for full dress, but of scarlet cloth. Trousers for light artillery men were reinforced in the seat and inner leg. According to General Orders No. 41 dated 10 May 1898, all light artillery personnel were to be armed with revolvers in russet leather holsters on waist belts with pouches, plus 13 light artillery sabres with belts, belt plates and slings for each battery of six guns.[97]

U.S. Regular Cavalry, Full dress

Cavalry officers wore the same pattern of dark blue, full dress frock coat, with the same insignia of rank, as for the other two main branches of service, but with the following differences. The buttons bore a spread eagle having a shield with the letter 'C' on its chest. The cloth ground of the shoulder knots was deep yellow, with the number of the regiment and insignia of rank embroidered in silver. Full dress helmets bore a gold cord and tassel, and a brass eagle plate with 'crossed sabre' insignia, and were adorned with a yellow buffalo-hair plume. Trousers were sky-blue with 1½ inch-wide deep yellow welts. Plain white duck or flannel trousers were permitted during the summer season. Pattern of 1886 top boots, of calfskin or enamelled leather, were worn on all mounted duty.

Cavalry officers carried the 1872-pattern sabre and scabbard suspended from a sword belt of black enamelled leather decorated with one broad stripe of gold lace for officers of field grade, and four stripes of gold lace, interwoven with yellow silk, and lined with black enamelled leather, for company grade officers. The overcoat was the same pattern as worn by officers of the other branches of service. Cavalry officers' capes were lined with yellow cloth.

N.C.O.s and enlisted cavalrymen wore the shorter-skirted Model 1888 dress coat. Fastened with a single row of nine regulation buttons, it had solid deep yellow facings on the collar, shoulder straps, cuff patches and coat tails. It was also piped around the coat front, skirt bottoms and side slits with deep yellow.

The full dress M1881 helmet for cavalry enlisted

men had gold cords and was topped with a yellow horse-hair plume. Insignia on the front consisted of a brass eagle plate with 'crossed sabres' and the number of the regiment in the shield. The leather chin strap was secured either end by small regulation 'crossed sabres' buttons. Trousers were of light-blue kersey with a reinforced saddle piece, of the same material, on the seat and inside legs. Welts on the trouser seams were the same as for the other branches, only in yellow.

U.S. Regular Cavalry, Undress

Collar insignia on the M1895 dark blue undress coat for cavalry officers consisted of two 1 inch-high crossed sabres of gold or gilt metal, or embroidered in gold, with the number of the regiment at the intersection. Shoulder strap insignia was the same as for the other branches of service, but on a deep yellow cloth ground. Undress cap insignia for officers was the U.S. coat of arms, as per other branches. A plain black leather belt was worn on undress duty. Undress trousers were the same as those for full dress. As with the other branches of service, a white duck or flannel coat of the same pattern, minus collar insignia or shoulder straps, was worn in hot climates.

The 9th Ohio Volunteers were one of the African American regiments raised as a result of the second call for volunteers issued on 26 May 1898. They are seen here drilling at Camp Alger, Virginia, where they were stationed from 20 May until 16 August 1898 as part of the Second Brigade, 1st Division, Second Army Corps. The NCOs' white cloth chevrons and trouser welts, plus that of the musician, can be plainly seen nearest the camera. John Sickles Collection.

Above and Opposite top.

There were two types of volunteer regimental flags – those bearing a state seal and arms like that carried by the 1st Regiment, California U.S. Volunteer Infantry (top), and the Federal eagle-pattern, similar to regular army units, like that borne by the 9th U.S. Volunteer Infantry (opposite). Ben K. Weed Collection.

U.S. Regular Cavalry, Field Uniform

The M1898 dark blue blouse for cavalry officers was the same as that worn by the other arms of service, except for the gold or gilt metal collar insignia, which featured two 1 inch-high crossed sabres with the number of the regiment at the intersection. The cavalry version of the khaki uniform prescribed for officers bore the same rank insignia as for other branches, and was faced with deep yellow on the collar, cuffs, and shoulder straps. Some blouses were also unofficially faced with this colour on the pocket flaps. These facings were reduced to shoulder straps only during August 1898. Khaki trousers for cavalry officers and enlisted men were reinforced in the seat and inner leg.

Enlisted men of the cavalry service wore the five-button, dark blue wool flannel sack coat, and M1895 cap with regimental number in upper angle and company letter in lower angle. Trousers were 'light sky-blue' kersey. Cavalry leggings were first issued in 1890. Made from drab, or light brown, canvas, they were 15° inches tall with laces passing through eight grommets and seven hooks. Canvas clothing, consisting of a sack coat and trousers of 6-ounce cotton duck dyed brown, had been issued for stable and fatigue wear since 1884. On active service in Cuba during June/July 1898, Regular cavalrymen in Wheeler's Division wore dark blue wool flannel shirts with sky blue trousers or, as in the case of the 10th U.S. Cavalry, light brown canvas trousers, drab leggings, and campaign hats with yellow wool hat cord. When eventually supplied, full khaki uniforms consisted of the same pattern of blouse as that issued to other branches of service, with yellow facings as per officers. N.C.O.s' chevrons were the same as for full dress, but of yellow cloth.

U.S. Corps of Engineers

Engineer officers wore the same pattern of full dress frock coat as other branches of service, fastened by gilt buttons with the time-honoured design consisting of an eagle grasping in its beak a scroll bearing the word

'Essayons', with an embrasured bastion surrounded by water, and a rising sun in the distance. Shoulder knots bore a solid silver shield, the same as for officers of the Adjutant General's Department, with a silver turreted castle, and were minus the aiguillette and shield.

The frock coat worn by enlisted men of the Engineers was the same as that for infantry, but with facings and N.C.O.'s chevrons of scarlet piped with white. Trousers were blue kersey, of the same pattern as for other foot troops, with scarlet welts piped with white for N.C.O.s. Enlisted men's helmets were the same as for other branches of service, with a white metal castle.

Engineer officers were distinguished by a silver-turreted castle beside the letters 'U.S.' on the collar of their M1898 dark blue undress blouses. The uniform was otherwise the same as for officers of other branches of service.

Before the adoption of the khaki uniform, engineer troops wore the dark blue wool flannel sack coat with dark blue trousers. Their M1895 undress cap bore a gilt metal castle with a company letter above it. When received via General Orders No. 168, dated 14 September 1899, khaki blouses worn by Engineers were faced with scarlet piped with white.[98] Drab campaign hats were presumably supplied to those engineer companies serving in the Caribbean and the Philippines.

Ordnance Department

Ordnance officers wore the same pattern of full dress as for other branches, with a silver 'shell and flame' insignia on the pads of their shoulder knots. Helmets also bore the silver 'shell and flame' device. Facings on enlisted mens' frock coats, and N.C.O.s' chevrons,

An 'H'-shaped cartridge belt plate worn by members of the New York State National Guard. Photo by the author/ courtesy of Dusan Farrington.

The 46th Separate Company, New York National Guard, was organised in 1888 and became Co. H, 2nd New York Volunteers, during the war with Spain. This company member wears a New York pattern sack coat with white worsted collar trim, darker blue trousers, white dress gloves and an 'H' plate bearing the initials 'NY'. His 'crossed rifles' hat insignia has the numerals '46' pinned above it. Anthony Gero Collection.

were crimson piped with white. Trousers were light-blue kersey with 1¼ inch-wide, crimson piped with white cloth welts for N.C.O.s. The 'shell and flame' insignia, of gold or gilt metal, was worn on the collar of the M1898 dark blue officers' blouse. Enlisted men of the Ordnance Department wore the standard pre-1898 sack coat and sky-blue kersey trousers. The M1895 undress cap worn by Ordnance Sergeants and Soldiers consisted of a metal 'shell and flame'. Via

Captain Peyton C. March wears the khaki uniform privately purchased for the Astor Battery by Colonel J.J. Astor. Note the additional facings on the pocket flaps, which may have set a trend followed by other early war units. March also sports a 'sun helmet', fine quality brown leggings and gauntlets. His hand rests on the wheel of one the six Hotchkiss mountain guns presented to the unit by Colonel Astor, who is seen inset top right. From 'Photographic History of the Spanish-American War' (1898).

General Orders No. 168, khaki blouses worn by members of the Ordnance Corps were faced with crimson piped with white.

Signal Corps

Officers of the Signal Corps wore the same full dress as other departments, fastened with gilt buttons bearing two crossed signal flags and a burning torch. The same device, in gold and silver embroidery, was displayed on the pads of the shoulder knots. They were also prescribed a shoulder belt and field glass case for dress and undress wear.

Sergeants of the Signal Corps wore the short-skirted Model 1888 dress coat, as per cavalry, with black facings piped with white, and white piping around the coat front, skirt bottoms and side slits. A First Sergeant of the Signal Corps was distinguished by three black chevrons and an arc of one bar, piped in white, enclosing crossed signal flags of red and white, and a burning torch in yellow. An ordinary sergeant wore the same, minus the arc. As of 24 April 1899, a corporal wore two chevrons enclosing the same device, a First Class Private displayed the device, without chevrons.[99] Trouser welts for sergeants of the Signal Corps were black and one inch in width.

The undress cap worn by enlisted men of the Signal Corps bore the crossed flag and torch device in white metal within an unburnished gilt wreath. Khaki blouses issued to enlisted men of the Signal Corps, via General Orders No. 168, were faced with black piped with white.

Hospital Corps

The Medical Department contained the Hospital Corps, founded in 1887, which numbered in 1898 about 700 soldiers specially recruited and trained in first aid, stretcher-bearing, ambulance service and ward nursing. Hospital corpsmen served in detachments at posts and with columns in the field.

Few U.S. volunteer units wore zouave uniforms during the Spanish-American War or Philippines conflict. The San Antonio Guard Zouaves, who formed Company G, 1st Texas Infantry, were photographed in camp at Jacksonville, Florida, during September 1898 in their zouave full dress. The 1st Texas served on garrison duty in Cuba from late December 1898 until March 1899. Their fancy trimmed jackets, baggy pantaloons and white waist sashes were probably reserved for special occasions and would not have been worn on active duty. Another unit from Texas called the Dallas Guard Zouaves mustered in as Company K, 2nd Texas Infantry. USAMHI/ photo by Jim Enos.

Captain Francis A. Cook, commander of the U.S.S. *Brooklyn*, flagship of Commodore Schley, wears the Model 1877 service coat with lustrous black mohair trim. His gold lace sleeve stripes were introduced in 1897. From 'Photographic History of the Spanish-American War' (1898).

The full dress uniform for Hospital Corpsmen consisted of a dark blue coat with emerald green facings (piped with white cord until 1897), and dark blue trousers with emerald green welts – 1¼ inch-wide for Hospital Stewards, 1 inch-wide for acting Hospital Stewards, and ½ inch-wide for privates. For full dress, Hospital Stewards were also distinguished by three chevrons and an arc of one bar, of emerald green cloth, inclosing a red cross attached to a patch of dark blue uniform material, on each coat sleeve. An Acting Hospital Steward wore the same omitting the bar. A Private of the Hospital Corps, and all persons 'Neutralized by the Terms of the Geneva Convention', wore a 'brassard of white cloth, 16 inches long and 3

Naval personnel engage in cutlass drill. The Midshipmen wear M1877 service coats, while the single strip of white tape around cuffs of the rating in the foreground denote the rank of seamen, third class. Note the adjustable strap on the back of his trousers. From 'Photographic History of the Spanish-American War' (1898).

inches wide, with a cross of red cloth, 2 inches long and 2 inches wide, in the center', to be worn on the left arm above the elbow. In 1897, Hospital Corpsmen were also prescribed bleached (white) cotton duck uniforms consisting of a sack coat and trousers when on duty in the wards. Khaki blouses received by Hospital Stewards via General Orders No. 168, dated 14 September 1899, were faced with emerald green.

Chaplains

The Army Chaplain could wear for full dress either a single-breasted, plain black frock coat fastened by nine black buttons, with standing collar; or a double-breasted frock coat of the same type of cloth, with falling collar, and two rows of seven black silk-covered buttons placed at equal distances. For 'undress', chaplains were required to wear either the black frock coat or a plain black sack coat of cloth or serge, with falling collar, and one row of five black buttons. Shoulder straps were the same dimensions as worn by the various arms of service, and had a ground of dark blue cloth, with a plain Latin cross of silver in the centre. A hat of plain black was prescribed for both full dress and undress. The overcoat was the same colour and cut as for other officers, but with plain sleeves. Trousers were plain black, without 'stripe, welt or cord'. Coats and vestments as required by the Church were worn over this uniform while conducting religious services.

Other specialist ranks

General Orders No. 38, dated 20 March 1873, established the new non-commissioned staff rank of Commissary Sergeant. This N.C.O. was assigned to military posts and installations to take care of the

These two ratings in blues from U.S.S. *Princeton* had their cabinet photo taken in Hong Kong in the 1890s, and were probably members of Admiral Dewey's Asiatic Station. The rating badge of the man on the left presents a puzzle, as it is of 1886–1897 pattern but is a Hospital Apprentice, first class, a rating not instituted until 1898. The bearded matelot on the right has a rating badge of the 1897 style, and is a Master at Arms, third class, with a specialty mark in the form of a star. Note the white cords around their necks, which were attached to the clasp knifes in the breast pockets. John A. Stacey Collection/photo by Robert G. Borrell, Sr.

Petty officer rating badge for a Sailmaker's Mate, 1st class, for white summer uniform. The eagle and specialty mark, a 'fid', were dark blue with chevrons of red felt, all on white cotton duck material. John A. Stacey Collection/photo by Robert G. Borrell, Sr.

This off-duty group of Marines wear a wonderful mixture of clothing. The man second from right, identified as 'Dawson, Co. E, 2nd Regt, 1898', has donned his M1892 special full dress uniform, with white linen summer trousers. The others wear M1898 summer field dress, with drab Mills belts and what appear to be cavalry-issue leggings. Note the stack of Lee rifles at the left. USAMHI/photo by Jim Enos.

many details related to the sustenance of the men.

Full dress for the Commissary Sergeant by 1898 still consisted of the M1884 single-breasted, dark blue frock coat fastened by nine general service buttons, and faced on collar, shoulder straps, and cuff patches with cadet grey piped with white. The coat front was also piped with white. Rank insignia for Post Commissary Sergeant consisted of three gold lace bars and a crescent with points facing to the front, placed 1¼ inches above the inner angle of the chevron. Trousers were the darker sky-blue introduced in 1885, with 1¼ inch cadet grey welts. The dress helmet was as per other branches of service, but with a staff eagle plate displaying a crescent overlay of white metal, or German silver, on its breast.

The 1895 undress cap bore a white metal crescent with points up, enclosed in a wreath of dead or unburnished gilt metal. General Orders No. 168, dated 14 September 1899, authorised Commissary Sergeants to wear khaki blouses with cadet grey shoulder straps piped with white, and same colour and pattern of chevrons as for full dress, only in cotton.

Post Quartermaster Sergeants wore full dress as above, with buff facings piped with white. Rank insignia consisted of three gold lace bars and a crossed key and pen. The eagle plate on the dress helmet also displayed a crossed key and pen. Trouser seam welts were buff and 1½ inches in width.

A silver crossed key and pen, enclosed in a wreath of 'dead' or unburnished gilt metal, made up the Quartermaster Sergeant's M1895 undress cap badge. Khaki blouses, issued to Post Quartermaster Sergeants after 14 September 1899, were faced with white piped with buff.

The rank of Electrician Sergeant was adopted in 1897. According to the Army Bill of 2 March 1899, one electrician sergeant was to be attached to each post garrisoned by coast artillery having electrical appliances.[100] This rank was distinguished by three red bars and a representation of forked lightning in white silk. Trouser welts were scarlet and 1¼ inches wide. Dress helmet eagle plates bore a symbol representing forked lightning, whilst undress caps carried the same device inclosed in a wreath. When specified in

September 1899, facings on the khaki blouse were scarlet.

As for previous wars, all U.S. enlisted men involved in military operations against Spain were entitled to a 'service in war' insignia consisting of a half chevron of gold lace piped in the same colour as the facings of the arm of service, to be worn on both sleeves above the elbow.

Musicians and Bandsmen

Musicians and bandsmen wore the same full dress uniform as other enlisted men of their respective branches of service, with braid of the same colour as the facings running across the breast, with the outer extremities terminating in a 'herring bone'. Dress helmets worn by band musicians bore a lyre of white metal. Undress cap insignia for field musicians was a bugle, with the number of the regiment in the centre, and the company letter above. That for band musicians was a white metal lyre. Trumpeters of cavalry wore a 'crossed sabres' insignia with the regimental number and company letter in upper and lower angles respectively. Full dress sleeve rank insignia of gold lace was as follows: Chief Musician, three bars and an arc of two bars, with a bugle in the centre; Chief Trumpeter, three bars and an arc of one bar, with a bugle in the centre; Principal Musician, three bars and a bugle; Drum Major, three bars and two embroidered crossed batons. The same insignia, only in branch colour cloth, was worn on the blue sack coat and khaki blouse.

U.S. Volunteers

The Regular Army was supplemented by additional 'Volunteer' units recruited to meet the needs of its expanding wartime role. More specialist troops – such as cavalry, engineers and signalmen – were required for the large-scale operations in Cuba and the Philippines. The Volunteer law of 22 April 1898 provided for 3,000 United States Volunteers to be organised and officered entirely by the Federal Government. Under this provision, the War Department raised three cavalry regiments in the western territories, the most famous being the 1st United States Volunteer Cavalry, more popularly known as the 'Rough Riders'.

General Orders No. 55, dated 26 May, authorised a further force of 3,500 U. S. Volunteer Engineers and 10,000 U. S. Volunteer Infantry. The former were organised into the 1st, 2nd and 3rd Regiments, U.S. Engineers, and each regiment was composed of 53 commissioned officers and 1,106 enlisted men. The officers were selected for their skill as military, civil, electrical, mechanical or topographical engineers. Enlisted men were recruited from 'every branch of the engineering profession and of mechanical skill'. The uniform worn by these units conformed to that 'prescribed for the use of engineer troops of the Regular Army'. They were armed and equipped as infantry.

Known as 'Immunes', the Volunteer Infantry were supposedly immune to tropical diseases. Organised into the 1st through 10th U.S. Volunteer Infantry, and commanded by Regular Army officers, five regiments were composed of white or Caucasian troops, and five of African Americans.[101]

A Volunteer Signal Corps, to consist of eight officers and 55 enlisted men for each division, was created a week later. The infantry units were intended to join the vanguard of the Cuban invasion, and were to remain as an occupation force after the fighting was over. The engineers and signalmen were needed as specialists in construction and communications.

A Marine lieutenant wearing the first pattern summer field uniform of brown linen. The Corps device and rank insignia may just be seen on his hat and collar respectively. John A. Stacey Collection/photo by Robert G. Borrell, Sr.

The Siege of Catubig, 15-18 April, 1900.

On 15 April 1900, a detachment of 31 men of the 43rd U.S. Volunteer Infantry, stationed at Catubig in the north of Samar Island in the Philippines, were attacked by some 600 insurgents armed with about 200 rifles and a cannon. Quartered in the town convent, the Americans held the place for one day, losing one man to the enemy's bullets. Early on 16 April, the insurgents set fire to the convent by throwing burning hemp from an adjoining church. Forced out into the open, a further 15 infantrymen were cut down as they tried to escape by river. The remainder dug in behind the blazing convent and held out against incessant enemy attack for a further two days. When a relief party reached Catubig, it found 13 of the intrepid garrison still alive, and about 200 Filipino Insurgents lying dead or wounded around them.

The painting depicts the U.S. infantrymen armed with Krag-Jörgensen rifles at the moment they broke out of the burning convent. The sergeant in the foreground has white facings on his khaki blouse, as per General Orders No. 168 issued on 14 September 1899. Others wear a mixture of dark blue overshirts and khaki trousers. Several have the 'Philippines' Eighth Corps badge pinned to their hats.

The Filipino insurgents wear a motley array of clothing combining some element of Western dress with styles of their own culture. Headgear includes turbans and antiquated helmets, while several men have also donned body armour. They carry a variety of captured firearms, plus their own traditional weapons and shields. Painting by Richard Hook.

1st U.S. Volunteer Cavalry, the 'Rough Riders'

The idea to recruit a band of drovers, ranchers and other westerners into a regiment of cavalry was first suggested to Assistant Secretary of the Navy Theodore Roosevelt by Baron Hermann Speck von Sternburg, later the German Ambassador to the United States. Hence, when the U.S.S. *Maine* blew up in Santiago Harbour in April 1898, Roosevelt already had a plan to raise such a mounted unit should the need arise. When offered the command of one of three volunteer cavalry regiments authorised by the Secretary of War later that month, Roosevelt fulfilled a long-cherished dream. But with little military experience, he wisely declined the colonelcy and urged that it be given to Dr. Leonard Wood, a Medal of Honor winner in the recent Frontier campaigns. Roosevelt was content with the lieutenant colonelcy.

Also known as 'Wood's Cowboys' and 'Teddy's Terrors', the regiment thus organised was probably the most heterogeneous unit ever raised in the history of American fighting forces. Its ranks were flooded with western cowboys, miners and trappers, Native Americans, New York policemen, big game hunters, Harvard ball players, actors, two of the nation's top tennis players, and even the marshall of Dodge City! The sons of the famous, including Micah Jenkins, son of the South Carolinian Confederate general killed at the Wilderness, and Charles Younger, son of bank robber Bob Younger, also joined up.[102]

Organised and mustered into service at San Antonio, Texas, Santa Fé, New Mexico and Muscogee, Indiana, between 1–21 May 1898, the 1st U.S. Volunteer Cavalry finally arrived at Tampa, Florida on 4 June. The recruits who gathered earlier in Texas wore a variety of civilian garb. Arizonians turned up with coloured hat bands which displayed in gold lettering: 'First Volunteer U.S. Cavalry – Arizona Column.'[103] Easterners arrived in 'sombreros and rough blue flannel shirts and each carried a valise containing linen and special brands of cigarettes, soap and razors'.[104]

By 14 May, each 'Rough Rider' was expected to obtain a canvas uniform, a campaign hat, a pair of brown leggings, one pair of shoes and a pair of socks. N.C.O.s' chevrons were to be of 'buff cloth', or light yellow, as were the seam stripes on their trousers.[105] The uniform thus acquired, for which each volunteer was reimbursed $7 by the U.S. Government, was a rather shapeless canvas cavalry stable, or fatigue, dress consisting of a sack coat and trousers made of six-ounce cotton duck dyed light-brown. Comparing the uniform of his own regiment with the 'canonical dark blue' of the Regulars with which it was brigaded, Theodore Roosevelt recalled: 'Our own men were clad in dusty brown blouses, trousers and leggings being of the same hue, while the broad-brimmed soft hat was of dark gray...'[106] Fastened by five buttons, which the 'Rough Riders' changed to the regulation gilt army pattern, the coat had a patch pocket on the left breast. One newspaper correspondent commented that these uniforms had the appearance of having been 'cut out with an axe'. A member of the regiment who wore what he called those 'stinking brown jeans' commented that the 'dye had a very sickening smell. It made us sick. By golly it was terrible. And they issued us the damned blue woolen shirts that almost killed with the heat. I wore mine tied around my neck most of the time.'[107]

Regarding the officers of this regiment, both Roosevelt and Wood purchased khaki cotton drill blouses and trousers, the former garment bearing

yellow facings on the collar and cuffs, as well as on the shoulder straps. On seeing the 'Rough Riders' arriving at Tampa, Private Post, of the 71st New York, recalled that Roosevelt's 'khaki uniform looked as if he had slept in it – as it always did'.[108] Other officers were photographed wearing more crudely-made cotton duck suits, minus facings, or the dark blue M1895 undress coat. During the assault on Kettle Hill and San Juan Heights, Theodore Roosevelt wore a sombrero attached to which was a blue polka-dot handkerchief, '*á la* Havelock, which, as he advanced, floated out straight behind his head, like a guidon'.[109] After this incident, the polka-dot handkerchief, or bandana, was adopted as the badge of the Rough Riders.

To ensure that his regiment was brigaded with the Regulars, Roosevelt used his influence in Washington to secure Krag-Jörgensen carbines and accompanying accoutrements for his troopers. War correspondent Richard Harding Davis, who accompanied the 1st U.S. Volunteer Cavalry, commented: 'Not one man in the regiment had ever fired a Krag-Jorgensen carbine until he fired it at a Spaniard, for their arms had been issued to them so soon before sailing that they had only drilled with them without using cartridges...'[110] Many also supplied their own favourite Winchesters and Colt .45s in open western-style holsters. During the action on 1 July 1898, Roosevelt carried a Model 1888 Cal. 38 New Navy Revolver salvaged from the sunken *Maine*! [111]

Detachments of the 'Rough Riders' were also armed with several unusual weapons. Sergeant Beekman K. Borrowe had command of 'a pocket-sized edition of the great dynamite guns of the USS *Vesuvius*'. Private Post described it as being 'completely self-contained and on wheels, with a trail and spade. It had two barrels, upper and lower. The lower was larger and into its breech one thrust a blank cartridge. When this cartridge was fired it pushed a piston, the piston compressed air, the air was released by a valve behind the dynamite projectile in the upper barrel, and the dynamite winged on its way somewhere up to a mile or so.' [112] This gun was later sold to the Khedive of Egypt. Lieutenant William Tiffany commanded two Colt automatic rapid-fire guns. All three of these weapons were used to great effect alongside the Gatling Gun Detachment during the attack on San Juan Hill, and subsequently in the trenches during the siege of Santiago.

State Volunteers

By the last decade of the 19th century, every state and most of the territories in the Union had a volunteer militia under command of the governor as commander-in-chief. This force could be called out to maintain law and order or to defend the nation against foreign invasion. Most of these organisations were called the 'National Guard', although variations included the 'Texas Volunteer Guard' and 'Georgia Volunteers'. Created by state law, militia company and regimental organisations were based on those of the Regular Army. Men enlisted for periods which ranged from three to five years, depending on what the state required. Continuing their civilian lives accept when called to duty, they devoted several days per month, and usually about a week in the summer, to training.

In 1897, the National Guard totalled about 114,000 officers and men, including 4,800 cavalry, 5,900 field and fortress artillery, 100,000 infantry, plus several thousand supply and service troops. The majority of this force lacked adequate military training. Less than half the states held regular instruction courses for their officers, and even fewer expected them to pass examinations for appointment or promotion. Enlisted men were required to attend weekly drills in their armouries, whilst regimental or brigade drills were held during a 7 to 10 day summer camp. On all these occasions, little attention was given to target practice, for which most states lacked ammunition, or to open order tactics more suitable for combat with modern rifles and artillery. Instead, instruction consisted mainly of close-order drill more suitable for parades and ceremonial purposes.

During the first few months of 1898, this force was supplemented by the volunteer movement. All across the nation, enthusiasts organised their own regiments, battalions and companies, some connected to the National Guard but many independent of it. Recruiting grounds were found among Republican clubs, labour union locals and student organisations. Millionaires offered to raise and equip units at their own expense. After the destruction of the *Maine* in February 1898, militiamen and volunteers flooded to the flag. The 'National Volunteer Reserve', established in New York on 25 March, enrolled about 15,000 men before its disbandment during the following month. Six hundred men in President McKinley's home town of Canton, Ohio, formed a regiment and declared their readiness to respond within 24 hours to any call for troops! According to Ohio officials, a total of 100,000 men from their state alone were prepared to offer their services had they been needed. The Adjutant General of Illinois told the press that his troops, numbering 7,500, could be *en route* for Cuba within 12 hours of a call.

Responding to public pressure and giving up its plans for an all-Regular wartime army, Congress authorised the President to raise a temporary Volunteer force of 125,000 men – the approximate strength of the National Guard – to serve for two years or for the duration of hostilities, whichever was shorter. Called out on 23 April, this force was to provide 22 regiments, 10 battalions and 46 companies of infantry; five regiments and 17 troops of cavalry; and 16 batteries of light artillery.

These State Volunteer units could adopt the same organisation, follow the same regulations, and receive the same pay and allowances as the Regulars. To accommodate the National Guard, any militia company, battalion, or regiment could volunteer as an entire body, and their officers were given Volunteer commissions corresponding in rank to those held in the militia. However, these officers had to pass a qualifying examination before receiving their commissions. Volunteer generals and staff officers were to be appointed by the President.

Virtually all the National Guard units turned volunteer were initially understrength due to lack of fitness, or unwillingness of peacetime members to enlist, but they quickly filled their ranks with new and more enthusiastic recruits. In approximately one month, 124,776 volunteers had taken the oath of enlistment. Nonetheless, long lines still formed outside the recruiting stations.

Who were the volunteers of 1898? An officer in the 6th Massachusetts Infantry described them as 'men from every walk of life... the lawyer, the mechanic, the laboring-man, the college student'.[113] Mostly single men in their early twenties, few underwent the test of battle, but those who did acquitted themselves well. Although not predisposed in favour of Volunteers, Captain John Bigelow, Jr., D Troop, 10th U.S. Cavalry, wrote of the 2nd Massachusetts Infantry on the march towards San Juan Heights: 'They were about as brown, and looked almost as hardy, as the Regulars. They went through mud and water, well closed up, at a good swinging gait.' After further observations in camp and on campaign, Bigelow commented that they 'were much better soldiers than Volunteers of our Civil War with the same length of service'.[114] John H. Parker, another Regular in Cuba, who commanded the Gatling Gun Detachment, praised the discipline and courage of the 'Rough Riders' and the 1st Illinois Infantry.[115]

Nonetheless, not every Volunteer proved to be an ideal soldier. Many Volunteer officers were lamentably ignorant about camp sanitation and neglected to inspect their camps, or failed to requisition much

needed supplies. Consequently, about 80 per cent of Americans who died in the war with Spain succumbed to typhoid, and most of those were from the ranks of Volunteer regiments. A few displayed rank cowardice. Of the advance towards San Juan Heights, Richard Harding Davis recalled: 'The inside story of the 71st New York is well known to every one who was present at the fight. The regiment did not run away, but it certainly did not behave well. The fault was entirely that of some of the officers. They funked the fight, and... refused to leave the bushes, and as a result the men either funked it too, or, as was the case with a dozen from each company, fell in with the regulars of Kent's division, and so reached the crest of the hill with them and led by their officers.'[116] During the Puerto Rico campaign, the colonel, the lieutenant colonel, the major and a captain of the 6th Massachusetts Infantry were dismissed from command for malingering on the transports or hiding in their tents while their regiment went into action.[117] To the credit of the Volunteers, of a total of 224,814 officers and men who served from April 1898, to July 1902, only 2,449 are listed as having 'deserted'.[118]

A second and final call for volunteers was issued on 26 May 1898, for a further 75,000 men to fill existing regiments and to form 22 new infantry regiments and 19 new artillery batteries. In mustering troops under this second call, the McKinley Administration paid particular attention to African American manpower. During the Civil War, 178,892 African Americans had served in the Union Army, more than a sixth of whom died in uniform. The Regular Army in 1898 contained only four Black regiments – two cavalry and two of infantry – whilst five of the new U.S. Volunteer Infantry regiments were to be Black. But the first 125,000 men recruited from the state forces included few 'men of color' because most National Guard units did not accept Black members. Through demonstrations and delegations to Congress and the White House, African Americans protested their exclusion from the Volunteer Army of 1898, and pleaded for the dubious honour of fighting for a country that denied them equality.

As a result, President McKinley accepted into service under the second call Black regiments from Alabama, Illinois, North Carolina, Ohio and Virginia. Furthermore, the first racially integrated regiment was raised in Massachusetts and, in a break with previous practice, several African American units were mustered in under officers of the same ethnic origin. For example, John R. Marshall, commanding the 8th Illinois Infantry, became the first Black colonel in the U.S. Army.

A Marine private wearing the khaki field dress officially prescribed as a summer uniform in 1900. Hat letter and numeral indicate Company C, 2nd Battalion, which landed in the Philippines on 21 September 1899. He holds a Krag-Jörgensen rifle, adopted by the Corps during 1899. John A. Stacey Collection/photo by Robert G. Borrell, Sr.

Regarding uniforms, National Guard units remaining within the limits of the United States were not required to make any changes to their dress, but wore 'the regulation uniforms of their State organizations'.[119] However, many of the uniforms, cartridge belts, knapsacks and other accoutrements in the possession of National Guard units were near disintegration from age. Hardly a single state had an adequate supply of tents, camp equipage or wagon transportation. The 1st and 2nd Louisiana were described by General Miles as being 'uniformed and equipped' only in part in camp at Mobile during May/June 1898.[120] On 13 June 1898, Major General William M. Graham, commanding the Third Division, 1st Army Corps, reported that the 9th Massachusetts, a regiment within his First Brigade, needed '4 rifles, 198 bayonet scabbards, 896 blanket bags, 41 canteens, 10 haversacks, 6 meat cans, 43 tin cups, 136 knives, 38 forks, 47 spoons, 29 pistols and

cartridge belts, 17 [pairs of] trousers, 108 leggings, 488 overshirts, 383 undershirts, 409 drawers.'[121] On 13 June 1898, General Graham advised that the 33rd and 34th regiments of Michigan Volunteers, also within his First Brigade, needed 'trousers, overshirts, and underclothing...', but were 'fully supplied with arms'.[122]

The supply of clothing and equipment to New York volunteers gathering at camps at Hempstead and Peekskill in May 1898 was delayed because legislation required that the State authorities should depend on convict labour for 'many essentials', instead of 'reliable military equipment houses...' Similarly, the majority of recruits received at the New York camps lacked 'instruction in the manual of arms' through lack of rifles.[123]

The 71st New York was mustered into Federal service at Hempstead, New York, on 10–12 May 1898. Prior to this, Colonel Francis Vinton Greene issued a circular to his command which stated: 'If ordered on active service, officers will wear campaign hats, plain blouse with brass buttons, belt over the blouse, revolver on the belt; mounted officers will wear boots, spurs, and buff gauntlets. Unless the order specifies that overcoats are to be worn, they will be packed with the officer's blankets. Enlisted men will wear campaign hats and the forage caps will be left in the armory.'

The same circular required that every man be provided with 'one blue flannel shirt (U.S. Army pattern), two suits of underclothing, two pairs of shoes, three pairs of socks, and toilet articles. Such articles as are not worn on the person will be carried in the pack. It is of the utmost importance that the shoes should be suitable for marching, of black leather, medium weight, stoutly made, with broad toes. A flannel band worn around the abdomen will be found conducive to health in active service.'[124]

Private Charles Post recalled of his uniform and equipment: 'Our shirts were a dark navy blue. A red bandanna was worn around the neck that served all purposes, and sky-blue trousers. Against any background we stood out in colorful relief. Now and then a canteen sprung a leak. A joint of bamboo was whittled out that held as much, and held it sweet – without that flavor of rusty iron and sowbelly which I still associate with our Civil War canteen. Our belts held fifty cartridges; in our socks (strung around the neck) were fifty or so more, and our haversacks held the remaining of the issue of two hundred. These were the old .45-70 cartridges.'[125] During the assault on San Juan Heights, Richard Harding Davis observed that some men of the 71st were 'lying on their faces about fifty feet below the crest, and as I passed among them on my way back I noticed that they wore in their hats the silver badge of the Seventy-First New York...'[126]

The pack mentioned in the above circular is a reference to the Merriam pack which, according to Charles Post, would have been ideally suited to carrying emergency supplies of whisky, had it not been so uncomfortable to carry. Post described it thus: 'Its center was about the size of the Civil War knapsack, which would hold just a quart bottle comfortably with some space left for socks, shaving materials, and a deck of cards or so. The blanket was formed into a long roll across the top of the pack and down each side. This blanket could accommodate three bottles, one atop and one each to port and starboard, and the pack straps held it securely so that every bottle was safe and well padded. Beneath the Merriam pack were two more straps. These were for one's rolled overcoat, which could accommodate another bottle or, better yet, a moderate-sized demijohn.'

However, Post concluded: '... the Merriam pack had two hickory sticks at each side fastened to the two upper corners of the pack. The other end fitted into the end pockets of a half-belt, which rested below one's kidneys. The Army believed that this took the load off a soldier's shoulders. We carried the Merriam packs on our kidneys, and the leverage of the sticks pulled our shoulders back so that we were perpetually being pulled back downhill with the swing of leverage in each stride. At Tampa, by official order, we abandoned the packs and went back to the old horse-collar blanket roll of the Civil War, invented by the men who had to wear them.'[127]

Mainly composed of National Guard units, the 1st New York Volunteers was shipped to the Hawaiian Islands for garrison duty during August 1898 wearing their state fatigue uniform. This consisted of a dark blue fatigue blouse fastened with five NY-pattern gilt buttons, and white worsted trim around the collar; and white duck or flannel trousers. For a parade or walking out dress, officers wore the all-white version of the M1895 undress coat, with the dark blue undress cap bearing the embroidered initials 'SNY'. The men wore the white Model 1888 summer sack coat and trousers of the Regular Army, with the M1895 undress cap, although most men chose to wear drab campaign hats, often with the numeral '1' stencilled on the crown.

The Astor Battery was organised in New York during May 1898, and set out early in the war for the Philippines. Commanded by Captain Peyton C. March, it consisted of six three-inch Hotchkiss mountain guns presented to the United States by Colonel John Jacob Astor. Each gun weighed 250

pounds and could be carried on mule-back over rough and precipitous terrain. The three officers and 98 men of this unit were some of the first to receive the khaki field dress adopted by U.S. forces on 9 May 1898. Privately purchased by Colonel Astor, their coats were not only faced with red on collar, shoulder straps, and cuffs, but also on the pocket flaps. Given the publicity received by the Astor Battery prior to departure, this may have helped to set the trend followed unofficially by so many other Volunteer, and Regular, units during the summer of 1898. With each man also armed with sabre, and .38 calibre revolver with a black rubber handle, the Astor Battery played a conspicuous role in the final attack on Manila on 12 August 1898.

U.S. Navy

At the beginning of 1898, the United States Navy possessed 53 vessels, consisting of four large modern iron clad battleships; two modern armoured cruisers; three heavily armoured protected cruisers; nine protected cruisers with medium armament; five lightly armoured cruisers; five old cruisers, or vessels with little or no protection; six second-class double-turretted monitors, 13 single-turretted monitors, five ships of 'little fighting value', one harbour defence ram and one dynamite gun vessel. This fleet was supplemented by 29 smaller vessels, consisting of torpedo boats, training ships, receiving ships and tugs.[128] As a result of the Navy Bill of 22 March 1898, the construction was begun on three new battleships, six torpedo boat destroyers and six torpedo boats. Also, it was determined that the total number of men and boys in Naval service was not to exceed 12,750 men and 1,000 boys.[129]

At the commencement of hostilities, the U.S. Navy was deployed as follows: the North Atlantic Station was commanded by Rear Admiral William T. Sampson; the Asiatic Station by Commodore George Dewey; the Pacific Station by Rear Admiral Joseph N. Miller; the Flying Squadron by Commodore Winfield S. Schley; the Mosquito Fleet, divided into seven Districts, by Commander Horace Elmer; the Northern Patrol Squadron by Commodore John A. Howell.[130]

Organisations of Naval Militia existed in January 1898 in 15 States, aggregating 3,703 petty officers and enlisted men, and about 200 commissioned officers. Just prior to the war, organisations were formed in two additional States and provisional organisations were formed in two others. When mustered in, officers and ratings were sent to the nearest receiving ship or station, from which details of men were drawn when needed. Regarding vessels for this Force, ten yachts and five tugs were purchased at a cost of $593,500, and the following vessels were fitted out for service in Southern waters, departing on 30 June 1898 – *Governor Russell*, *East Boston*, *Apache*, *Viking*, *Sylvia*, and later *Potomac* and *Kanawha*.

The U.S. Naval officer needed at least four or five different coats ranging from the 'special full dress, full dress, social full dress, frock and service dress, besides caps, chapeaux, helmets, gloves, boots and shoes of the best quality of special designs'. According to the *Army and Navy Journal*, the 'wearing apparel of a Lieutenant was figured at $1,365, that of an Ensign was fixed at about $1,050, and the Rear Admiral's at about $2,000'.[131]

The tailed-body coat worn for special full dress in 1898 was similar in many respects to the first blue and gold full dress coat adopted in 1802. Made of Navy blue cloth, it was double-breasted with two rows of nine Navy buttons, a standing collar, two and a half-inch deep cuffs and two pointed pocket flaps in the tails. Regarding collar decoration, only an admiral and vice admiral wore oak-leaf and acorn embroidery, while a rear admiral was distinguished by a one-inch strip of gold lace. A captain bore a strip of 1½-inch wide gold lace around the top and down the front, and a ½-inch wide strip around the bottom, of the collar. A commander wore ¾ inch-wide lace; a lieutenant, one inch-wide strip.

Regarding sleeve lace on the tailed-body coat, an admiral and vice admiral were permitted to wear the elaborate oak-and-acorn motif, while a rear admiral was distinguished by a band of two-inch wide gold lace with a ½-inch strip above it. A commodore wore a single two-inch wide band. A captain had four strips of ½-inch lace, and commanders three. A lieutenant commander wore two strips of ½-inch lace with a ¼ inch strip between them, and a lieutenant, two strips of ½-inch lace. An ensign wore a single strip of ½-inch lace. By May 1899, a special sleeve insignia had been re-introduced for Admiral Dewey. Previously worn by Admiral David Dixon Porter, it consisted of two strips of two-inch lace with a one-inch strip between them. All wore the five-pointed star of the line above this. Staff officers of the same relative rank wore the same insignia, minus the star.

The black cocked hat, or *chapeaux*, was bound with black silk lace, with a tassel showing at the fold each end, formed of five gold and five blue bullions. On the cock, or front, of the hat was fastened a black, five inch-diameter silk cockade. Flag officers wore over this a 'loop of six bullions, the center two twisted', while all other officers entitled to wear cocked hats

had a loop of four bullions.[132] A tail coat for evening social dress was authorised in 1873. Cut to the waist in front, it had five Navy buttons either side. Epaulettes were optional, while sleeve lace was the same as for special full dress.

The frock coat was the multi-purpose coat of the Navy. It generally followed the pattern of the undress coat introduced in 1852, except that by 1898 it was longer. This garment was worn with epaulettes, cocked hat and gold-laced trousers for full dress; and with epaulettes, plain blue or white trousers, and either a cocked hat or a white helmet for dress. For undress, it was worn with the cap.

Gold-laced trousers, worn with both special full dress and full-dress frock coat, were decorated with lace of the same width as that worn on the collars of the special full-dress coat. All officers from commodores through commanders wore one-inch trouser lace. All with the rank of lieutenant commander through ensign, ½-inch lace. Staff officers wore a strip the same width as line officers with whom they held relative rank.

Originally introduced in 1877, the service coat was worn by all commissioned officers and midshipmen who had graduated from the Naval Academy, plus cadet midshipmen and cadet engineers. Made of dark navy blue cloth or serge, it was single-breasted, with fly front, fitted with plain flat gutta-percha buttons. It had 1¼-inch wide lustrous black mohair braid on the front edge, around the bottom, and up the back seams. The standing collar was also trimmed with the same material. Beside this at a distance of ⅛ inch was a ⅛ inch-wide black silk braid.

Introduced in the 1830s, the Navy blue cloth cap worn by all commissioned officers since 1886 had virtually no overhang, the top being just about the diameter of the head. The cap device prescribed earlier for all officers, in 1883, consisted of 'a silver shield, emblazoned paleways, of thirteen pieces, with a chief strewn with stars surmounted by a silver spread eagle, the whole being placed upon two crossed foul anchors embroidered in gold'.[133] Gold embroidery was introduced to the cap visor in June 1897. Visors of caps worn by rear admirals, commodores, captains and commanders were covered with dark blue cloth. All other commissioned officers wore caps with black patent leather visors. Visors of caps of line rear admirals and commodores were embroidered all over with oak leaves and acorns. Staff officers of corresponding rank had a ½-inch wide band of gold embroidery around the front edge and back of the visor. Line captains and commanders had a border of oak leaves and acorns on the front edge only, while staff officers of corresponding rank had a ½-inch wide band around the front.

Since 1886, first class petty officers had worn a double-breasted sack coat with two rows of four buttons, lapelled collar, a single, flapped pocket on the left breast, and two pockets of the same pattern either side below the waist. Their cap device was the same as per the regulation Navy button, and consisted of a spread eagle perched on a stock of a horizontal anchor, surrounded by a circle of 13 stars. Other petty officers wore the same blue overshirt, tucked inside the trousers, as prescribed for enlisted men.

Petty officers' rating badges, including 15 specialty marks, were authorised on 24 September 1894, as a result of the creation of the new rating of chief petty officer. Insignia for this rank consisted of a chevron of three stripes with point down, and a single arc attached to the upper stripe, with a spread eagle resting on the centre at the top of the arc with head turned to the right. A Petty Officer, 1st class, wore the same minus the arc; a Petty Officer, 2nd class, only two stripes below the eagle; and a Petty Officer, 3rd class, the same with a single stripe. Specialty marks were worn between the eagle and the stripes. The eagle and specialty marks were in white cloth on blue clothing, and in blue on white. On both blue and white uniforms the chevrons, and chief petty officers' arc, wore red cloth. These rating badges were worn on the right arm for the starboard watch, and the left for the port watch.[134]

Since 20 January 1876, all enlisted men had worn blue overshirts with three rows of white tape ³/₁₆th of an inch wide on the collars, with a white star, purely for decorative purposes, at the corners. The traditional black silk neckerchief was always worn under the collar. The number of strips of white tape around the cuffs denoted a man's class. Three strips indicated petty officers, first, second and third class; ship's cooks, first and second class; seamen, hospital apprentices and bakers, first class. Two strips were used to identify seamen, second class; ship's cooks, third and fourth class; hospital apprentices; and bakers second class. Seamen third class and mess attendants had a single strip. Ex-apprentices below the rank of first class petty officers a specialty mark below the neck-opening of the jumper – white on the blue uniform, and blue on white. First class petty officers wore theirs on the lower sleeve of their coat. Since 1886, the watch mark for ratings below chief petty officer were indicated by a thin white stripe around the shoulder seam, the side dependant on the watch.

The dark blue sailors' round cap came into use at the beginning of the Civil War, and seamen began to ornament them with a black silk ribbon. By the late 1880s these ribbons bore the name of the vessel on which the wearer served. Leggings worn during land action were drab canvas with covered lacings.

Pea jackets, worn by enlisted men since 1886, consisted of a thick Navy-blue woolen double-breasted jacket, with two rows of five large gutta-percha buttons, rolling collar and two vertical front pockets. Sou'westers were worn by all crew on deck during foul weather.

Service whites were the only uniform suitable for warm-weather wear. An officers' white cap, or white cover over the blue cap, had been worn since 1873. A white tropical helmet and white service coat was introduced in 1883, with shoulder straps showing officers' rank and corps added three years later. Photographic evidence suggests the latter were often not worn in combat during 1898–1902. In line with provision for officers, first class petty officers were permitted to wear a white duck sack coat after 1886. The white jumper and trousers worn by enlisted men was patterned after that in blue, but the jumper was worn outside the trousers, as opposed to being tucked in. The collar and cuffs of this garment were covered with thin Navy-blue flannel, the former bearing the same striped border and stars as worn with the blues. The watch stripe was dark blue. The white canvas hat had been warm weather headgear since 1886.[135]

The use of steam for propulsion and machinery aboard ship had created the need for a working uniform, and since 1869 enlisted personnel had worn a pair of overalls and a jumper of white cotton duck.

The sword worn by U.S. Naval officers had changed little since its introduction in 1852, having a slightly curved and etched blade. Its fish skin grip was wound with twisted gilt wire. The guard and pommel were of gilded brass, the latter having a so-called Phrygian helmet with a top covered by a separate cap bearing an eagle in a circle of 13 stars. The knuckle bow was often decorated with dolphins' heads and floral designs, and contained the raised letters 'U S N' on a ribbon set within a spray of oak leaves and acorns. Scabbards varied from black leather or fish skin, to blued metal, and possessed two carrying rings.[136]

Gold-embroidered sword belts were officially to be fastened by the 1876 Pattern 'false' two-piece plate bearing an eagle perched on a horizontal anchor surrounded by 13 stars. However, contemporary photographs indicate that officers continued to wear the two-piece 1852 pattern.[137]

Boarding parties and those seamen involved in land actions during the years 1898–1902, carried the Lee Navy rifle, a high velocity, clip fed, bolt-action .236

calibre arm using smokeless powder. The possible number of these weapons in Navy hands is indicated by the fact that the Ames Sword Company, of Chicopee, Massachusetts, had furnished '20,000 Navy bayonet scabbards and throgs [sic]' by the end of August 1898, and was working on 10,000 more.[138]

The Navy cutlass had a large brass guard handle, polished steel blade, with leather scabbard and brass stud for attaching to the belt by a sword frog. Seamen also had a clasp knife for everyday use with a metal ring on the butt of the handle, through which a white cord or tape was passed. The looped end of the latter was worn around the neck, and the knife was carried in a left breast pocket of the overshirt.[139]

U.S. Marine Corps

The U.S. Marine Corps was increased to the unprecedented size of 119 officers and 4,713 enlisted men following the outbreak of war with Spain. Commanded by Colonel Charles Heywood, the Corps provided 40 ships' detachments, and manned 15 shore stations, as well as fielding one expeditionary battalion to Cuba under Lieutenant Colonel R. W. Huntington, and another to the Philippines in 1899 led by Colonel P. C. Pope, which by 1900 had grown into the 1st Marine Brigade, consisting of two rifle regiments and two artillery companies.[140]

Prescribed via the 1892 Regulations, special full dress for the Marine Corps comprised a single-breasted dark blue cloth tunic trimmed with scarlet braid, with eight large-size buttons bearing an eagle perched on a fouled anchor within an arc of 13 small stars. Shoulder knots were scarlet, as were the pads which bore the 'fouled anchor and globe surmounted by a spread eagle' set within a brass crescent. Adopted in 1868, this emblem borrowed the globe from the Royal Marines, but showed the western, instead of eastern hemisphere, and added the American eagle and maritime anchor. Trousers were sky-blue with red welt for officers and NCOs, and headgear consisted of either a black cloth-covered helmet with brass spike, bearing a silver metal 'anchor, eagle and globe' plate, or a plain white cloth-covered helmet for warm weather service.[141]

At the beginning of the war with Spain, the undress or field dress of the Marine officer consisted of a service coat of dark blue cloth trimmed, as per the M1877 Navy pattern, with lustrous black mohair. The Corps device and insignia of rank were worn on the collar, ¾ of an inch apart, the latter being backed with a scarlet cloth patch. Trousers were sky-blue with 1¼-inch wide scarlet welt. Headgear consisted of the M1895 undress cap, adopted by the Marines in 1897, of dark blue cloth with a band of 1¼-inch wide black mohair braid within the cap welt. A knot on top of this cap was composed of four double loops of ½-inch black silk braid. The visor of black patent leather had a bound edge, and was lined with green leather. The silver metal Marine Corps cap device was worn at the front, with a gold chin cord. Trousers were sky-blue with red seam welts.

The undress sword belt was of white patent leather, from which was suspended the Marine officers' Mamaluke pattern sword, with sword knot of russet leather. Also attached was a russet leather holster with the letters 'U S M C' stamped on the flap, within which was carried the Navy .38 calibre revolver.[142] Subsequent service in the Philippines represented the first overseas expedition in which Marine officers were directed to leave their swords behind and to arm themsleves only with revolvers.

Marine enlisted men wore a dark blue indigo flannel cloth sack coat, piped down the front, around the base of the collar, shoulder straps, straps for belt, and cuff tabs, with one-eighth inch scarlet cloth. NCOs' rank was indicated by yellow edged red inverted chevrons, and red welts down the seams of their sky blue trousers. Undress caps were plain dark blue with black leather visor and chin strap, and Marine Corps device at the front. All ranks also wore plain white linen trousers (part of an all-white summer fatigue uniform adopted in 1894), and white linen cap covers, in warm weather. Trousers were tucked into drab canvas leggings of Navy pattern with covered lacings. Equipments consisted of the M1895 Navy-issue dark blue webbing Mills belt with black leather pouch flaps. Arms consisted of the 6mm. Lee straight pull rifle, adopted by the Marine Corps in 1895, attached to which is an 8½-long bayonet. This was exchanged for the Krag-Jörgensen rifle in 1899.[143]

The blue wool field dress was abandoned by the Marine Corps sometime between 10–14 June 1898, and a brown linen summer uniform, including a five-button blouse with rolling collar and two flapped breast pockets, was adopted for use by both officers and men. This was worn with a felt olive drab campaign hat, and blue wool, or white linen, shirt. Obviously prompted by their service in the Caribbean and the Pacific, the Corps completed their warm weather uniform change via the 'Regulations of the Uniform Dress... of the Marine Corps, 1900', which included a khaki field dress consisting of a single-breasted blouse, with standing collar, pointed cuffs, shoulder straps, and two flapped breast pockets with box plaits.[144]

Cuban Revolutionary Forces

The size of the 'Liberating Army of Cuba' varied between 25,000 and 40,000 soldiers, dependent on the circumstances and the changing military situation. Created in 1868 at the beginning of the Ten Years War, it was nick-named the *mambises* after the followers of Juan Ethninius Mamby, a fighter for Dominican independence from Spain. With the outbreak of further revolution in Cuba on 24 February 1895, this force was commanded by Maximo Gomez, a Dominican and ex-Spanish officer, and was organised into six Divisions, each commanded by a General of Division, who was responsible for campaigning in one of the six provinces of Cuba. Antonio Maceo, Lieutenant-General of the Liberating Army, commanded the Division in Pinar del Rio. Portioned off by the big *trocha*, or trench, from the rest of Cuba, this region constituted the Department of the West. Aguierre commanded in Havana, Jose Lacret Morlot

Cuban Revolutionaries, or *mambises*. Note the two men standing in the foreground wear what appears to be officers' rank insignia – the man on the left has several stars on his coat lapel indicating he is a general or staff officer, whilst the man on the right displays three small stars on a leather swatch pinned to the front of his shirt. He also wears a Cuban national flag emblem attached to his hat, as do most of the men formed in the rear. From 'Photographic History of the Spanish-American War' (1898).

A company of unusually well-armed Cuban infantry, commanded by Major Estrampa. The mounted officer and two dismounted officers brandish machetes. Note the national flag at right, and the bugler at left. A small bugle, wrapped with red cords, is preserved today in the *Museo de la Ciudad* in Havana. From 'The Story of the Spanish-American War and the Revolt in the Philippines' (1898).

in Matanzas, Carillo in Las Villas, Suarez in Camaguey and José Maceo in Oriente. During 1896, Calixto García landed at Baracoa and, as ranking general, took command of Camaguey and Oriente, thus creating the Department of the East.

Each division consisted of two or three brigades, commanded by Brigadier-Generals. Each brigade consisted of from three to four regiments, and a regiment comprised from three to four troops, or companies – also known as *fuerzas*, or force. The latter were nearly all cavalry, and operated in districts where both officers and men had always lived and were well known. Two troops constituted a squadron, with a maximum strength, including non-commissioned officers, of 100 armed men, or *armados* (bearers of long arms, rifles or shot guns). In districts where horses were scarce, a company would by necessity contain a percentage of infantry. The officers of a

mounted squadron, or a full company of infantry, of local forces consisted of a Major, a Captain, two Lieutenants and an *Alférez* (derived from the old Castilian title of honour, 'standard-bearer'), four Sergeants and eight corporals. Several squadrons, or an unusually larger force, operating together were commanded by a Colonel or Lieutenant-Colonel. Every unit was allowed by regulation to muster *desarmados*, or camp followers, such as orderlies, servants and cooks, to one-fourth of its strength of armed men. Every squadron was supposed to muster a blacksmith, but in provinces such as Matanzas and Las Villas there was a great scarcity of horseshoes and nails, whilst in Camaguey the softness of the forest roads made such measures non-essential.

These local forces were supplemented by the expeditionary regiments which were recruited generally through the island and contained Spanish deserters, or volunteers who had arrived on expeditions from abroad. Usually detailed to accompany general officers on their criss-cross marches across provinces and districts, one such unit was the *Orientales*, an Afro-Cuban infantry regiment commanded by Quentin Banderas. Every general officer was entitled to an *escolta*, or personal bodyguard, to number from 40 to 80 men, who were usually expeditionaries appointed to his service.

The ability of these Cuban insurgent leaders won the respect even of European professionals. Waging a campaign of raids and ambushes, and avoiding large-scale battles, one of their major aims was to destroy Cuban agriculture, especially the sugar industry, which was the chief Spanish source of revenue on the island. Hence they burned cane fields and farm buildings, and in their raids killed many planters or drove them into the Spanish-held townships. When the situation demanded it, local squadrons and companies came together to harass Spanish garrisons, ambush supply columns, or capture and destroy isolated enemy outposts. These actions were made possible by an excellent intelligence service which enabled the *mambises* to avoid major Spanish columns with ease. A force of almost 5,000, including artillery, was several times assembled in eastern Cuba, where Spanish garrisons were thinly spread, in order to attack small towns.

To keep order in areas they controlled, and to provide their army with food and equipment, the *mambises* created a civil government under President Salvador Cisneros Betancourt on 19 September 1895. Elected and mainly dominated by the army, this organisation encouraged the establishment of small gardens, and the keeping of herds of cattle, in remote places where Spanish troops did not patrol. It also set up crude workshops, especially in the eastern provinces, in order to make shoes, saddles and accoutrements, and to repair weapons, many of which were captured from the Spanish. Despite these efforts, the *mambises* often ran short of food, ammunition, clothing and medical supplies, whilst their families subsisted under the most primitive conditions in remote hideaways in the hills and mountains.

According to an eye-witness account, General Maximo Gomez, military commander of the *mambises* forces, was described as being 'a straight little white-bearded man, in a gray cloth suit and riding boots, with two gold stars on either lapel of his coat...'[145] Another source reported: 'He wore an ordinary soft hat of grey felt with a Cuban coat-of-arms, such as were sold in New York for ten cents, pinned to the front. Suspended from his waist is a Moorish style scimitar.'[146] The *Museo de la Ciudad* in Havana preserves a jacket worn by Gomez. Made of white linen, it was fastened by hooks and eyes, not buttons, and has a low standing collar. Miniature cloth Cuban flags form its shoulder straps, and it has four pockets without flaps – the one on the left breast having a vertical opening. Also preserved are 15 brass and iron five-pointed stars worn at various times as rank badges

by Gomez.[147]

General Jose Lacret Morlot, of Haitian French descent, was described as being 'exceedingly neat in his costume, his belt and leggings were always well blacked, he carried a change of linen uniform in his saddle-bags... The most extraordinary article of his dress was the tall Mexican hat... It had a silver star within a triangular crimson cockade on one side, and from it a long red cord hung about his neck and down his back like an artilleryman's aigulette.'[148] Major General Bartolomeo Maso wore a dark blue pillbox cap with the Cuban arms embroidered on the front. Quentin Banderas sported a pair of gold worsted shoulder knots, while his uniform seems to have been embellished with some form of gold braid.

As a general rule, other officers of the 'Liberating Army' wore coats, jackets and pants of white duck, '...which, being the clothing of the country, really constituted the uniforms of the insurgents, so far as they could be said to have any. All officers were provided with appropriate insignia of rank, and wore on their hats the tri-colored Cuban badge.'[149]

The only form of rank insignia prescribed for use by *mambí* officers involved a system of stars worn on the collar by general and staff officers, whilst field and company grade officers, and N.C.O.s, wore either embroidered or painted stars, or chevrons, respectively on the front of their *bandoleras*, or shoulder belts. In theory, a major-general wore three gold, or yellow, stars on each collar; a general of division, two; a brigadier-general, one. A colonel wore three yellow stars on his shoulder belt; a lieutenant-colonel, two; and a *comandante*, or major, one.[150] According to eye-witness accounts and sketches of Grover Flint, this system was used quite extensively, if not strictly adhered to. Flint observed the rank of major was sometimes indicated by two stars on a leather swatch attached at right angles to the belt.

Regarding company grade officers, the rank of captain was given by three white stars on the shoulder belt; that of lieutenant by two white stars; and an *alférez*, one. Flint recounted the approach of 'a lieutenant distinguished only by a star on his crossbelt'.[151] Each of the aforementioned rank insignia from colonel down was to be attached to a branch service coloured patch secured in turn to the belt – that for infantry was green; cavalry, red; artillery, light grey. To what extent this practise was adhered to in the field is not known.

The rank of First Sergeant was sometimes indicated on the cross-belt by three white half chevrons; that of Second Sergeant by two; and a Corporal, one half chevron.[152] A photograph of a

Two machetes of the type used in Cuba during the 1890s. The example on the left was probably made in either the U.S. or Britain, although the English maker's mark is too worn to properly decipher. The hilt is made of almost black horn. The more decorative example on the right was made in Germany by Jacob Büngersohn in Bremen, but was clearly for export to a Spanish-speaking country, as there is a lion on the locket and an eagle on the chape. Conrad Cairns Collection.

Cuban N.C.O. in the Guanabacao Museum in Cuba shows rank insignia consisting of very large chevrons and arcs sewn to each sleeve, as per U.S. regulations for a sergeant major.

A number of cloth badges of rank, some quite complex, survive in the museums of Cuba. One has a large cloth star with a small metal one in its centre. Another has a red cloth star with a smaller white star sewn on top of it, which in turn has a blue roundel in its centre. Lieutenant Rafael Agosta Dominguez wore a cockade consisting of three triangles – blue, white, and red – with a small white star in the centre triangle made from the bases of the three joined together.[153]

A few Cuban officers carried swords. That belonging to Antonio Maceo is now in the *Museo del Ejército* in Madrid, and consisted of a British 1796-pattern light artillery sabre. José Wu, a Chinese-born

Comandante, carried what appears to have been a Spanish sabre, but the national weapon of Cuba, used by both infantry and cavalry, as well as their officers, was the *machete*. The hilts of these weapons were usually of horn or wood, with blades either curved or straight, and often equal to the length of a full sword. Some surviving examples were made in the U.S. and Germany, and one preserved in the *Museo de la Ciudad* has a particularly fancy eagle-headed pommel. Others were of much more crude workmanship. All were worn high on the left hip from a frog attached to the waist belt. Scabbards could be brown or black leather, with or without metal fittings.[154]

Regarding clothing for enlisted men, coats and trousers were made from cotton drill bought in the villages by Government agents. The tailoring was done by the peasant women, under the direction of the local official, or prefect. The garments were then taken to the *mambí* camps to be issued, with other supplies, to the most needy. According to Grover Flint: 'Then the barefooted men, the men without shirts or trousers, the hatless... assemble in expectant line and continue to clamor until the last equipments are distributed.'[155] The Afro-Cuban insurgents, or *Orientales*, were more scantily clad, wearing 'scarcely more than a gunny-sack, held about the loins by a cartridge belt, with the merest remnant of a shirt, or pair of trousers'.[156]

A variety of shoulder arms were carried by the *mambises*. Surviving examples include a shotgun, a percussion blunderbuss, a U.S. M1873 'Trapdoor' Springfield, a Winchester carbine, an 1887 'Marlin Safety' carbine (Winchester action), a Spanish made M1871 Remington, a 7mm Mauser repeating carbine and a Spencer carbine. Grover Flint commented on seeing 'the usual assortment of Winchesters, Remingtons, and Spanish Mausers' when he encountered a force of 60 *armados* near Cardenas.[157] He also provided a graphic account of the work of the largest Cuban Government workshop, at Mayari in Las Villas Province: 'Within the main building are work-tables and benches in rows, with racks for tools and arms in course of repair. Fifty men are employed in cleaning and repairing carbines, pistols, and machetes. They are well supplied with screws, rivets, and the minute machinery of firearms. There is a furnace with a bellows, and tanks for bronzing long arms and even cannon. An old carbine that has seen hard service may be brought here and fitted with bands, screws, and breech-block, freshly bronzed and stocked, and sent back to the owner nearly as good as new. Gun-stocks are turned out by hand in the wood-carving department, of beautiful red and yellow woods, each stamped with the initials "P. y. L.," standing for "Patria y Libertad" (Fatherland and Liberty).'

Flint also observed: 'The lower end of the hall is devoted to the repairing of machetes. Handles of beautiful design are made and harmoniously fitted to the various styles of machete, from the long, pointed Camaguey blade, to the broad forester's cutlass and Santo Domingo scimitar. The handles are made from layers of ox horn, heated and shaped with brass forms, and pressed over night in a vise. They are then clinched with brass rivets, trimmed with knife and file and polished to their utmost brilliancy.'[158]

Regarding ammunition for the insurgents, there was always a shortage. Charles Post, of the 71st New York in Cuba, recalled: 'The Mausers the insurrectos captured were excellent weapons, but there was no ammunition for them – beyond the beltful unbuckled from a dead Spaniard.' According to Post, the prostitutes of Havana and other cities supplied the *mambí* with Mauser cartridges. In return for their favours, an ordinary Spanish private soldier would be charged 100 cartridges; an N.C.O. 200 cartridges; and an officer, a box of 1,000 cartridges. Post concluded: 'At night a friend of the prostitute would call. He had a load of wood or charcoal or sugar cane, or some

wine. When he left, his saddle pads would be lined with Mauser bullets.'[159] Until the American invasion of Cuba, the *mambí* depended on gun running through the Spanish coastal patrol boats for ammunition for their artillery, and for rifles other than the Mauser.

The flag carried by the insurgents, which was adopted as the national flag of Cuba on 20 May 1902, was designed in New York City during June 1849, by a Cuban exile in the filibuster 'army' of Narciso López. It was described in a broadside distributed among López's volunteers in April 1850, as consisting of 'the Tricolor of Liberty, the Triangle of Strength and Order, the Star of the future State, and the Stripes of the three departments of Cuba'.[160] The National Flag raised at Demajugua on 10 October 1868 consisted of a field containing a white bar over a blue bar with a red canton bearing a single white star. On 10 April 1869 it was replaced by a similar flag with a field containing three blue bars and two white bars.

The *Museo de la Ciudad* in Havana has an impressive collection of about 30 flags from the period. The largest measures about 10 feet on the fly

A Cuban flag captured at Paso Real, and donated to the *Museo de la Infanterio* of Spain in 1896 by General Agustin Luque y Coca, who commanded the Holguin Division of the Spanish Army on Cuba in 1898. Museo del Ejército, Madrid.

by 6 feet on the staff. Most are of plain rectangular national pattern, although some are swallow-tailed. Three exceptions include a flag with the inscription 'LEGION COLUMBIONA' on its white bars; a plain headquarters flag, with its coloured field now faded, bearing in white letters the designation 'CUARTEL GENERAL / E L / 5° CUERPO', with a white star in the centre between the 'E' and 'L'; a swallow-tailed lance pennon of 1868 national pattern.[161]

Both Generals Gomez and Lacret were reluctant to fly flags on active service, but preferred to have them packed away in a staff officer's saddle bag. They were only displayed on grand occasions, when a 'flag-pole' was cut and a trooper detailed to carry it. Various miniature forms of the flag were worn pinned to the hats of Cuban insurgents during the period 1895 through 1898. Others appear to have worn a single small star hat insignia.

Paulina Ruiz carried the flag of Brigadier-General Pancho Perez, commander of the Santa Clara division. Wearing a linen coat and a knee-length skirt that showed a pair of trousers of cotton drill with narrow blue stripes, she rode by the side of Pancho Perez during at least two machete charges against guerilleros. From Grover Flint, 'Marching with Gomez' (1897).

Spanish Forces

On the eve of war with the United States, the Spanish Army consisted of two distinct elements – the Peninsula, or Home, Army, and the Colonial Army, or Army of the *Ultramar* territories. Both these forces became involved in the conflict in 1898.

The Home Army consisted of Active Units and the Reserve. The Active Units in turn were composed of the Standing Army and the Depot troops. The Standing Army was made up of eight army corps, each of which was based on a military region, or district, in Spain. The 1st Corps encompassed New Castille, Estremadura, Segovia, Avila, Toledo, Ciudad Real, Badojos and Cacéres; the 2nd Corps – Sevilla, Granada, Cordoba, Huelva, Cadiz, Jaen, Malaga and Almeira; the 3rd Corps – Valencia, Castellon de la Plana, Alicante, Murcia, Albacete and Cuenca; the 4th Corps – Catalonia, Barcelona, Gerona, Kerida and Tarragona; the 5th Corps – Aragon, Saragossa, Huesca, Ternel, Soria and Guadalajara; 6th Corps – Burgos, Navarra, Alaba, Guipuzcoa, Biscay, Santander and Logroño; 7th Corps – Old Castile, Valladolid, Palencia, Salamanca, Zamora, Léon and Oviedo; the 8th Corps – Gallicia, Corunna, Lugo, Orense and Pontevedra.[162]

As a result of the Conscription Law of 14 February 1882, all Spanish males attaining the age of 20 were in theory required to serve a term of 12 years in the Home Army – six years on the Active List and six years on Reserve. However, due to a poorly funded Treasury, the Spanish Government could not afford to fully operate this system. Hence, the annual draft of conscripts was selected by lot, the remainder being dismissed and classed as 'Available Recruits'. Those selected for military duty, also known as 'men of the first class', were not obliged to serve in the ranks for the full six years, but during the third year were sent home on unlimited furlough, and classified as the 'Active Reserve'.

The wealthy classes could avoid conscription altogether on payment of 2,000 *pesetas*, whilst exemption was granted to government and municipal employees, eldest sons of widows, fathers over the age of 60 'on legally binding themselves to support their parents', men convicted of felony, and those physically or mentally unfit for service. A further relaxation of the law in favour of the wealthy was granted by the admission of 'one-year volunteers', while considerable privileges were accorded to young men studying for a profession, who were allowed to select their regiment, to sleep out of barracks, and to take part only in 'the technical portion of military work', thereby avoiding all routine or fatigue duties.[163]

With mobilisation for war in 1898, the thinly-manned regiments of the Standing Army were brought up to war strength by recalling from furlough the men on Active Reserve, whilst Available Recruits were required to make themselves ready to replace casualties.[164]

Recruiting for the Colonial Army was carried on primarily by means of voluntary enlistment. If recruitment fell short by this means, numbers were made up by a fresh draw on 'the men of the first class' originally conscripted for the Home Army. Recruits served a term of four years in the Colonial Army, reckoning from the date of embarkation, and a further four years in the Reserve. Exchange was freely permitted among recruits belonging to the home and colonial service, the sole restriction being that both parties must belong to the same military district. Substitution into colonial service was permitted on condition that the substitute was 35 years of age and free from all personal liability to other military service.[165]

The Colonial Army consisted of the Army of Cuba, the Army of Puerto Rico and the Army of the Philippines. By the beginning of 1898, 150,000 regular soldiers of the Home Army had also been committed to Cuba to suppress insurrection. This force was supplemented by the enlistment of an additional 80,000 Cuban loyalist 'Guerrillas' and 'Volunteers'.

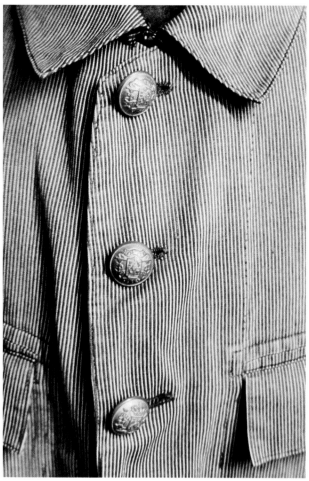

Examples of *rayadillo*, or fine-striped, campaign uniforms worn by Spanish troops in Cuba and the Philippines. The jacket worn by Captain Santiago Ramón y Cajal, of the *Sanidad Militar*, or Medical Health Department, shows the type of cloth issued after 1885, which had a white stripe on a blue base. Note his brass buttons bear the letter 'S' superimposed on the letter 'M'.

The jacket worn by infantry officer Lieutenant Colonel Julián Fortea Selvi, is typical of the *rayadillo* worn by 1898, having darker blue stripes. Museo del Ejército, Madrid.

Eight thousand Spanish regulars were also present in Puerto Rico, whilst the Philippines contained 26,000 more. Meanwhile, a further 150,000 troops were standing ready back on the Iberian Peninsula.

The Colonial Army of Cuba was poorly trained, and many of its officers knew little of the tactics and technical skills involved in modern warfare. Mainly composed of young conscripts who received little training other than rudimentary drill, the rank and file were ill-prepared for the irregular war they had been sent to wage. American artist Frederic Remington commented in 1897: 'The raw material of the Spanish army is good, but they have been demoralized, and their officer corps leaves much to be desired. They have a good rifle, carry 200 rounds of ammunition, and are good marchers, but they are defective in commissariat and rarely march over two days from their base. The insurgents "pot" into the head of the columns, whereat they halt, bunch up and rain badly aimed Mauser bullets. They form hollow squares when menaced by cavalry, and generally their tactics are obsolete, but inspite of this the enlisted men stand the "gaff" much better than they ought to be expected to considering their hollow leadership.'[166] Leonard Williams, a British observer of the conflict, wrote: 'It makes one sad to see the quality of the expeditions packed off in heartless shoals to Cuba, boys, to look at, at fifteen or sixteen, who have never held a rifle till this moment, and now are almost ignorant which end it fires, good lads – too good to go to such uneven butchery – with cheerful, patriotic, willing faces, but the very antithesis of a soldier.'[167]

The effectiveness of the Spanish Army was further weakened by disease. Between 1895 and 1898, over 13,000 men died of yellow fever, whilst on the eve of the American invasion an estimated 25 to 30 per cent of Spain's soldiers lay sick in hospitals.[168] Nonetheless, the Spanish Army gained the respect of many Americans. On 3 July 1898, Theodore Roosevelt wrote to his friend Henry Cabot Lodge of the battle at

San Juan: 'We have won so far at a heavy cost; but the Spaniards fight very hard and charging these entrenchments against modern rifles is terrible.'[169]

The military district of Cuba was divided into six provinces consisting of Havana (within which was located the capital), Villas, Santiago de Cuba, Puerto Principe, Matanzas and Pinar del Rio. The supreme commander, or general in chief, of the Spanish forces in Cuba was Captain General Ramon Blanco y Erenas, Marques de Pena Plata. He was supported by aids-de-camp consisting of three lieutenant colonels, one major and two captains of infantry; two majors of cavalry; and one captain and first lieutenant of engineers. The Second-in-Command of the district, who also served as inspector-general of all arms, was General of Division Julian Gonzalez Parrado. His aids-de-camp amounted to one major of infantry; and captains of cavalry and artillery respectively.

The Staff of the General Headquarters was composed of a Chief, namely Lieutenant General Luis Manuel de Pando y Sanchez, and Second-in-Command, Brigadier General Enrique Solano Llanderal. The Corps of the General Staff of the Army consisted of a colonel, two lieutenant colonels,

two majors and three captains. The Captain General also had his own General Staff containing a second-in-command, Colonel Julio Alvaraez Chacon, plus a lieutenant colonel, four majors and three captains. This hierarchy was also supplemented by the General Headquarters of the Inspector of Artillery, and of Engineers; plus a Field Park staff, Military Medical Service, Department of Military Instruction, Mechanical and Pyrotechnical establishments, a Commandery of Engineers and staff of various Military Hospitals.[170]

On the eastern end of the island around the capital, the Division of Havana was commanded by General Parrado, and consisted of three brigades containing a total of 12 infantry battalions, one rifle battalion, 22 squadrons of cavalry, eight companies of fortress artillery and one telegraph company. The Division of Pinar del Rio under General Francisco Fernandez Bernal contained one large brigade made up of 10 infantry battalions, one battalion of marine infantry, three squadrons of cavalry, one railway company, one transport company and two telegraph companies. The Matanzas Division, commanded by General Louis Molina de Olivera, consisted of six infantry battalions,

The *jipijapa* hat, with national cockade, worn by Captain Santiago Ramón y Cajal, of the Medical Health Department.

Detail showing stiffened muslin cockade and brass button bearing the royal coat of arms. Museo del Ejército, Madrid.

Above.

A very rare study of Spanish NCOs and enlisted men in campaign dress enjoying rest and recreation in Havana prior to the American invasion. At least six men wear the loosely attached NCOs' stripes on their lower sleeves. The man pouring wine wears a barracks cap, or *gorro de cuartel*, while several others proudly sport the national cockade in their straw hats. Wisconsin Veterans Museum.

Opposite.

Spanish riflemen in Cuba in 1898. The fine stripes on their *rayadillo* campaign uniforms are indiscernable at this distance. All three hold M1893 Mauser rifles, and two have their sword bayonets fixed. They all wear *jipijapa*, or straw hats. Note a fourth man is sat on the floor virtually out of shot holding his hat to show the national cockade, which was not usually worn on campaign duty. Their belt plates bear the rifle regiment bugle horn insignia with the numeral '5' inset, which may indicate they belonged to the 5th Tarifa Rifle Battalion, serving with the Trocha Jucaro-Moron Brigade. Wisconsin Veterans Museum.

two battalions of mobilised volunteers, one battalion of marine infantry, two cavalry squadrons and one section of mountain artillery.

The central region was garrisoned by three divisions which had responsibility for manning the *Trocha*, or 'Great Ditch', composed of a depression between two ranges of hills of about 20 miles in width, consisting mostly of swampy land which divided Cuba in two. The Santa Clara Division, under General Ernesto de Aguirre y Bengoa, contained three brigades totalling nine infantry battalions, one rifle battalion, at least four squadrons of cavalry, one section of mountain artillery, one telegraph company and three transport companies. The Sancti Spiritus Division, led by General Juan Salcedo Mantilla de los Rios, had three brigades containing 10 infantry battalions, two rifle battalions, 12 squadrons of cavalry,

three half batteries of mountain artillery, four transport companies and one company of sappers and miners. A separate command called the Trocha Jucharo-Moron Brigade, commanded by Colonel Arturo Alsina Netto, consisted of four infantry battalions, two rifle battalions, five railway companies, six companies of sappers and miners, one transport company and a section of telegraphers.

The eastern end of the island was controlled by four further divisions. The Puerto Principe Division, under General Adolfo Jimenez Castellanos, contained four infantry battalions, three squadrons of mounted rifles, one section of mountain artillery, one transport

Spanish Solbiers

A Spanish sun helmet plate surmounted by a metal cockade.
Ben K. Weed Collection.

**An enlisted man's painted metal cockade. The red loop
indicates it was worn by a cavalry trooper.** Ben K. Weed
Collection.

company and one company of sappers and miners. The Santiago de Cuba Division, which did most of the fighting in 1898, was commanded by General Arsenio Linares Pombo, and possessed one brigade with additional units attached, amounting to 12 infantry battalions, one battalion of mounted rifles, four squadrons of cavalry (including lancers), one battalion of mountain artillery, two transport companies, three companies of sappers and miners and a telegraph company. The Holguin Division, under General Agustin Luque y Coca, contained two brigades, plus the 'Light Division', and totalled 12 infantry battalions, three rifle battalions, two marine infantry battalions, two squadrons of cavalry and one battery of artillery. The Manzanillo Division, commanded by General Juan Arolas Esplugues, had two brigades totalling 13 infantry battalions of infantry, three rifle battalions, two squadrons of cavalry, two batteries of mountain artillery, three transport companies and a telegraph section.

This force was supplemented by a 'Corps of Public Order', at least nine battalions, or *tercios*, of Guerillas, plus three battalions of mobilised volunteers consisting of infantry and artillery, and a disciplinary brigade responsible for military punishment.

As Puerto Rico had achieved a level of autonomy and home rule by 1898, the garrison on that island was much smaller. Commanded by Lieutenant General Manuel Macias Casado, who was supported by staff officers of the Central Bureau, and General Staff of District, the Puerto Rico force consisted of 3 provisional battalions; 2 rifle battalions; an infantry battalion; a battalion of fortress artillery, attached to which was two batteries of mountain artillery; four mounted squadrons, plus two foot companies, of Civil Guard; a telegraph company; and one 'Public Order' company. This was supplemented by 14 volunteer rifle battalions and a volunteer cavalry squadron.[171]

Spanish troops in the Territorial Division of the Philippines by 17 May 1898, were commanded by General Fermín Jáudenes y Alvarez, and consisted of seven regiments of native infantry, 15 'expeditionary' battalions organised in Spain and sent to the islands to assist in the suppression of the insurrection; one native cavalry regiment; one expeditionary cavalry squadron;

one regiment of fortress artillery; one regiment of mountain artillery; a regiment of native engineers; one company of marine infantry; a single ordnance detachment; three *tercia*, or regiments, of native Civil Guard; one detachment of native *Carabineros*, or custom guards; a native train, or transport, unit; a sanitary detachment, plus at least 12 companies of militia and guerrillas.[172]

Since 18 August 1886, the Spanish infantry of the line of the Peninsula Army had worn for full dress, daily use and campaign duty, a dark-blue jacket called a *guerrera*, of deep blue, or *azul turqui*, which had two breast pockets and was fastened by a single row of seven metal buttons. A jacket of similar cut had been adopted by the artillery by 1891. The cavalry were wearing a double-breasted version after 1892, while the dragoons acquired a single-breasted jacket of similar style in 1897. Trousers were full-cut, of madder red for infantry, dark blue for rifles and artillery, and either sky or deep blue for cavalry.[173]

Full dress headgear consisted of a distinctive military cap, with stiffened crown and top sloping from front to back, called a *ros*, which was first adopted by the Spanish Army during the 1850s. A smaller version of this cap, called the *Leopoldina*, after General Leopoldino O'Donnell, had been introduced by the 1890s. A fuller, softer cap, very similar to that worn by the French Army, and called the *Teresiana*, was also worn by 1884.

A heavy dark blue wool greatcoat, or *capote*, was an essential part of the European campaign dress. It is doubtful Peninsula regiments sent to Cuba took this garment with them. If they did, it would have been reserved for formal inspections, reviews and social occasions, and would not have been used in the field. Footwear consisted of *zapatos*, or half boots, of black leather. Also worn for undress were *alpartagas* or hempen sandals consisting mainly of soles with slight counters and toe pieces, tied above the ankles with black material ribbons. These were usually worn over white stockings, but occasionally with bare feet in warm climes.

Spanish troops in the colonies had worn a light-weight summer uniform of linen, or *lienzo*, since the 1770s. This became the multi-purpose uniform for the Colonial troops of Cuba when full dress was abolished in the Colonies on 3 June 1876, subsequent to the Royal Decree of 11 June 1874. This Law appears to have been extended to the garrison on Puerto Rico via the Royal Order of 8 October 1880.[174] On 11 November 1892, the same style of campaign uniform as described in the Decrees of 1876 and 1880 were extended to the troops in the Philippines.

Spanish accoutrement belt plates. (top) The 73rd Jolo Infantry Regiment, originally the 6th Regiment of Native Infantry, served on Luzon Island in the Philippines. (bottom) The 30th Alfonso XIII Rifle Battalion. Ben K. Weed Collection.

The colonial uniform prescribed in 1876 consisted of a coat of blue striped drill with gilt buttons, and trousers of brown drill. By the 1890s, the latter were of the same cloth as the coat. An exact description of the type of cloth used in these campaign uniforms has not been found. During the mid-19th century it was referred to as being of *hilo listado azure*, or blue striped thread. By the end of the century it was known as *dril azul rayado* (blue striped drill) or *coleta azul rayado*, which was possibly a reference to a local type of cloth indigenous to Cuba, and used by the workers and general population of the island since the 1840s. The earliest types of cloth used seem to have had light blue stripes which were more widely separated, whilst surviving examples of uniform jackets and trousers from the 1890s have thinner stripes of a darker hue, known contemporaneously as 'the cloth of a thousand stripes', or *mil rayas*.[175] Seen from a distance, this material looked either very light blue or blue/grey, and after several washes seems to have faded to almost white.[176] Its appearance when viewed from different

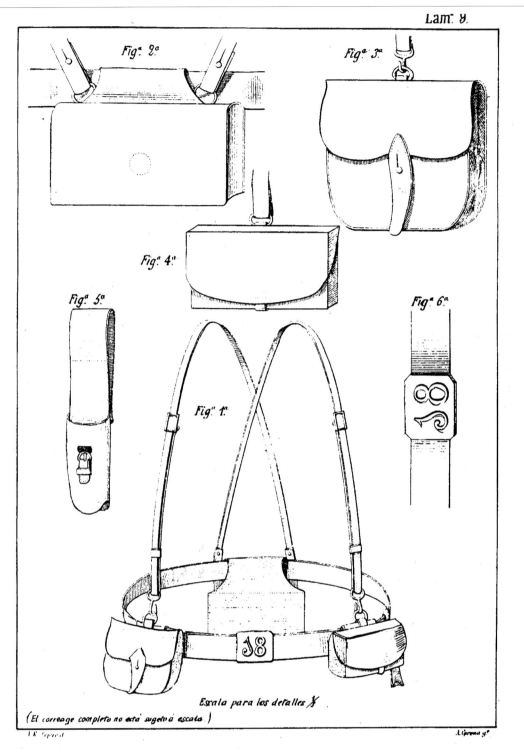

A plate which accompanied the 1886 Uniform Regulations showing the basic accoutrements worn by the Spanish infantryman and rifleman. Courtesy of René Chartrand.

distances is reflected in several eye-witness accounts. During 1895, Grover Flint recalled seeing Spanish troops at a distance and commented: 'The gray line of Spaniards was now within easy range.'[177] Given the opportunity afforded by closer range at San Juan Heights on 1 July 1898, Private Post of the 71st New York observed: 'Just beyond the shed, two dead Spaniards sprawled in their thin, blue-and-white pin-striped uniform – like pajamas [sic] to us...'[178] Theodore Roosevelt recalled of the same occasion: 'When we reached the trenches we found them filled with dead bodies in the light blue and white uniform of the Spanish regular army.'[179]

These fine-striped *rayadillo* uniforms were worn for daily use with detachable branch service facings on the collar and cuffs. These were usually removed for campaign duty, and would definitely have been taken off for washing in order to prevent non-fast colours from running! For the same probable reason, NCOs' sleeve bars of yellow or red were only loosely tacked to

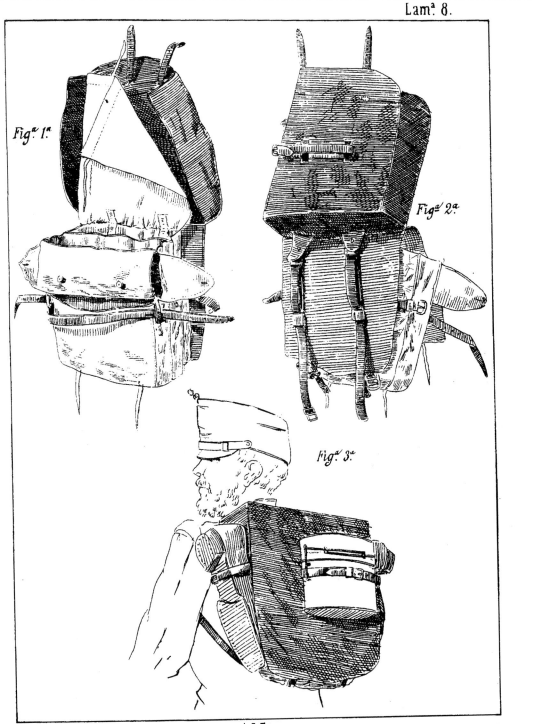

Fig.ª 1.ª

Fig.ª 2.ª

Fig.ª 3.ª

A. R. Tejero.

A plate from the 1886 Uniform Regulations showing the knapsack carried by Spanish infantryman and rifleman.

Courtesy of René Chartrand.

the sleeve at either end.

Headgear for campaign duty, also officially prescribed in 1876, consisted of a wide-brimmed straw hat, or *sombrero*, of finer *jipijapa* for officers and coarser *yarey* for enlisted men, with cockade in the national colours worn on the right side of the crown. According to the artwork of Frederic Remington, these hats were often worn with the brim pinned up on either two or three sides, giving the effect of either a bicorne or tricorne hat.[180] Cockades were either made from cloth or painted metal, and were usually removed for campaign duty. For everyday duty, the *Leopoldina* cap continued to be worn, with a white linen cover and 'havelock' when necessary. Barracks caps, or *gorra de cuartel*, of dark blue cloth, or *rayadillo*, were also donned for everyday wear. Sun helmets, or *capacete*, covered with white cotton, similar in shape to the M1880 helmet issued to the American army, and bearing a metal plate displaying the Royal Coat of Arms under a crown and cockade, were worn by

A selection of Spanish military coat buttons: (top row – left to right) **Royal Arms in relief – maker, 'Superfin, Paris'; Royal Arms in relief – maker, 'Jennens, London'; Royal Arms with Pillars of Hercules and 'Infanteria' in scroll below – maker, 'T. W. & W., Paris'; Army School of Recruits, or** *Escuela recuitas* **(found in Havana), 'E R' cypher – maker, unknown;** (second row – left to right) **Civil Guard (found in Cuba) – Royal Arms with letters 'G C' in ornamental script either side – maker, 'T. W. & W., Paris'; Municipal Guard (found in Havana), arms of the City of Havana, with letters 'G M' in ornamental script either side – maker, 'T. W. & W., Paris'; Royal Arms with letters 'O P' either side – maker, 'T. W. & W., Paris'; Army, Engineer officer (found in Cuba), castle, crown and wreath – maker, 'P. Fue e Hijos, Madrid & Barcelona';** (third row – left to right) **Artillery, crossed cannons – maker, 'J. Fue, Barcelona'; Artillery, Cannoneer (found in Cuba), with 'Bombero' on plain surface – maker, unknown; Cavalry, Lancers, two crossed pennons – maker, 'T. W. & W. Paris'; Cavalry, Lancers – maker, unknown;** (fourth row – left to right) **Army, Sappers & Miners, with crown above two crossed mattocks, heads up, with a spade perpendicular between them (found in Cuba) – maker, 'Scovill Mfg. Co.'; 1st Infantry Regiment, with italic '1' (found in Cuba) – maker, 'T. W. & W., Paris'; 1st Infantry – maker, unknown; 1st Infantry – maker, 'T. W. & W. Paris';** (fifth row – left to right) **2nd Infantry – maker, 'Adolfo Gaza, Barcelona'; 2nd Infantry (found in Cuba) – maker, unknown; 3rd Infantry; 3rd Infantry – maker, 'T. W. & W. Paris';** (sixth row – left to right) **3rd Infantry; 3rd Infantry (found in Cuba) – maker, unknown; 3rd Infantry, with ornate '3' – maker, 'Adolfo Gaza, Barcelona'; 4th Infantry – maker, 'Lieferanten'.**
Ben K. Weed Collection.

colonial troops in Puerto Rico and the Philippines.

Buttons and accoutrement plates worn by both Peninsula and Colonial armies were supplied by a number of makers, including Lugas Saenz, of Madrid; P.N. Feu, of Madrid and Barcelona, and Adolfo Gaza, of Barcelona. The main suppliers in the colonies were Peil Cabello, at Havana, and Adolfo Roensch, of Manila. Foreign suppliers included Trelon, Weldon & Weil, of Paris, and the Scovill Manufacturing Company, based in Waterbury, Connecticut.[181]

The Spanish riflemen on San Juan Hill in July 1898 possessed a much better firearm than his American counterpart. Indeed, General Breckenridge commented in 1899 that 'the bravery of the Spanish soldier fighting on the defensive is beyond doubt, and the Mauser rifle "an excellent and rapid weapon," while the smokeless cartridge adds to its special efficacy'.[182]

The Spanish Army began small scale trials with a few Turkish-pattern Mauser rifles in 1887, but did not seriously consider using the weapon until 1891, when the Royal Decree of 2 December of that year authorised the 6th Saboya Infantry Regiment and the 19th Puerto Rico Provisional Battalion to carry the M1891 rifle calibre 7.65 x 53mm. The M1892 rifle, basically a 7mm calibre Turkish-pattern weapon, was

adopted by Spain on 30 November 1892, and about 30,000 of these were ordered by 27 August 1893. During the same period, about 10,000 M1892 Mauser cavalry carbines were acquired. However, very few of the former were ever delivered due to the advent of the improved M1893 rifle.

Adopted by the Spanish Army on 7 December 1893, the calibre 7 x 57mm 'smokeless' M1893 was probably one of the best known Mauser rifles of all time. The first Mauser to feature a 5-round, charger-loaded magazine, enclosed entirely in the stock, the lower portion of its bolt face was squared in order to more easily facilitate the feeding of cartridges. The clip guides were milled into the front of the receiver bridge, and the safety catch could be applied only when the action was cocked. A V-notch leaf rear sight was graduated to a maximum range of 2,000 meters. A bayonet lug on the bottom of the upper barrel band facilitated the use of the Model 1893 sword bayonet. A swivel-ring attached to the lower band, and another on the bottom of the buttstock, provided for a carrying sling. An initial order was made for 251,800 of this

model, and by 1896 its production had begun at the National Arms Factory at Oviedo, in northwestern Spain. The Spanish were so pleased with the M1893 rifle that they awarded Paul Mauser the Grand Cross of the Order of Military Merit.

In use in various forms since 1893, but not officially adopted by the Spanish Army until 7 May 1895, the M1895 Mauser carbine was fully stocked to the muzzle, had a turned-down bolt handle, and a sling bar and ring on the underside of the stock at the

Top.
The Spanish Model 1893 Mauser rifle.

Middle top.
Detail showing bolt closed.

Middle below.
Detail with bolt open.

Bottom right.
Manufacturer's markings on the left side rail. This weapon was made by Ludwig Loewe & Co. at Berlin.

Bottom left.
Detail showing rear sight and straight bolt handle. Courtesy of the Ministry of Defence Pattern Room/photos by the author.

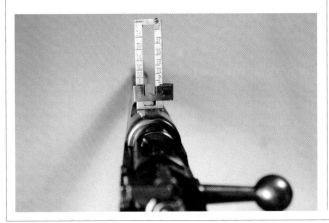

Sun helmets are much in evidence as this Spanish unit, headed by a regimental band, march away from the quayside at Manila. The plates on their helmets are just visible. Museo del Ejército, Madrid.

wrist. Firing a five-round magazine, its sight was the same as found on the M1893 rifle with a maximum effective range of 1,400 meters.[183]

The M1870 Remington Rolling Block rifle, made at Ilian, New York, was officially adopted by the Spanish Army on 24 February 1871, although the Colonial Army in Cuba had been in receipt of earlier versions of the weapon since 1867. With three screw-clamping bands, it had a small back sight with the leaf hinged at the rear of the attachment block. The cleaning rod protruded beneath the muzzle, and a socketed bayonet locked around the front-sight base. With manufacture beginning at Oviedo in 1871, and at the Euscalduna works at Planencia in 1872, this calibre .43 weapon was modified in 1889 to take the new 11mm cartridge developed by Lieutenant Colonel Luis Freire y Góngora and Captain José Brull y Seoane. Known thereafter as the M71/89, the Remington rifle remained the standard Spanish rifle for many years, and was still carried by many volunteer units during the conflict in 1898.

The manufacture of Remington cavalry carbines was begun at Oviedo in 1870/71. Officially adopted on 24 February 1871, the 11 x 58mm calibre M1871 Remington carbine had a half-stock held by a single screw-clamping band and a small back sight on the barrel. Swivels underneath the band and buttstock were accompanied by a ring on a bar attached to the left side of the receiver. The Remington Artillery carbine, or musketoon, was adopted on 23 December 1874 to equip the engineer corps and garrison artillery. A variant of the M1871 rifle, it had two bands, a small carbine-type back sight, and carried the M1874 socket bayonet. About 1,500 Remington Dragoon carbines were produced at Oviedo for use with Spanish cavalry in 1889.[184]

Spanish officers were usually armed with revolvers, such as the six-shot Lefaucheux or the Model 1884 Smith and Wesson, carried in leather holsters on the waist belt, being attached to a black worsted cord worn around the neck.[185]

Since 1886, Spanish infantry accoutrements for the Remington rifle consisted of a black leather waist belt secured by a yellow metal plate bearing the regimental number or bugle horn, depending on whether the unit was a Regiment of Line Infantry or a Rifle Battalion. A leather cartridge box was carried either side at the

This unusually well-accoutred Spanish infantry regiment composed of Filipinos, commanded by Spanish officers, carry their knapsacks with blanket rolls strapped around the outside. The complete absence of shoes suggests they preferred to serve in bare feet. Note the native NCO and battalion or company flag on the right. Museo del Ejército, Madrid.

front. That on the right held two tin inserts each containing 20 rounds standing upright in the upper sections which were withdrawn by the soldier as needed. When this supply was exhausted the man pulled up the two inserts and removed from the lower sections two packages containing 20 reserve cartridges. These he opened and placed in the upper sections. The cartridge box on the left contained two further unopened packages of cartridges. A third box worn on the rear of the belt contained further tin inserts packed with more cartridges. With further ammunition carried in his knapsack, it was possible for each man to carry 200 rounds. When loading the rifle, cartridges were always taken from the right hand box, which was replenished when necessary from the left and rear boxes, or from the knapsack.

This accoutrement belt was supported by two adjustable leather shoulder straps attached to belt rings via metal hooks, which crossed at the back and were secured to the belt either side of the rear cartridge box via a loop and two further metal rings.[186]

Later belts used included the Mauser leather waist belt with three small flapped pouches in front, each of which carried a clip of five rounds, and a larger pouch at the back carrying further clips of ammunition. This was often worn reversed with the larger pouch at the front. This belt could also be worn as a bandoleer.

The infantry knapsack, or *mochila*, consisted of an inner bag, or *morral*, made from polished canvas, with an outer cover of soft, black calf skin which gave protection from inclement weather. The outside flap of the latter was strengthened with board to serve as a table, and was closed by two leather straps which buckled at the bottom of the bag. A mess tin was strapped to the centre of this flap. On top of the outer cover was a pouch of dressed sheepskin, secured with two straps and buckles, which could carry four extra packages of cartridges. The inner canvas bag was partitioned to keep food separate from clothing, and carried the following items: in the largest compartment, one cap, two shirts, two pairs of underpants, one towel, two handkerchiefs, one toilet bag, brushes and a jacket; in the second compartment, eating utensils and one day's rations, which

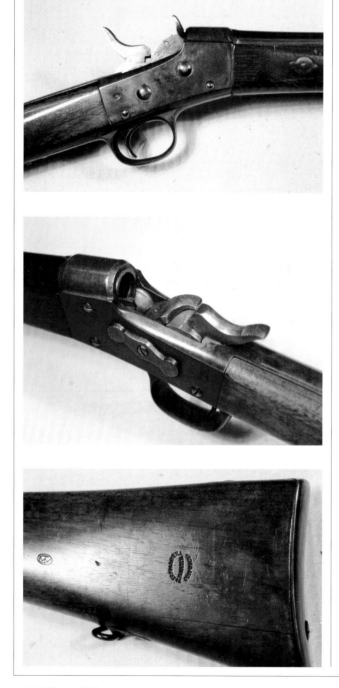

Top.

A Model 1871 Remington rifle manufactured at the Euscalduna works at Planencia in Guipuzcoa.

Middle.

Detail showing the 'Rolling Block' breech. The essence of this system lay in a sturdy hammer and a radial breech piece. Rolling blocks were opened by thumbing the hammer back to full-cock and pulling on a finger spur to rotate the breech to gain access to the chamber. After loading, and the breech piece had been returned to the closed position, a pull on the trigger dropped the hammer. As the hammer fell, shoulders ran forward under the breech piece to make it secure.

Bottom.

Detail of buttstock showing manufacturer's markings – **'F. EUSCALDUNA/PLANENCIA/GUIPUZCOA.'** Courtesy of the Ministry of Defence Pattern Room/photos by the author.

supplemented those carried in the mess tin. Another strap, passing through loops either side of the inner bag and through slits in the outer cover, was buckled around items carried outside the knapsack, such as a pair of shoes, and a blanket or greatcoat. Leather carrying straps, padded at the top to prevent chafing, passed over the shoulder and under the arm pits, fastening by means of a gilt metal buckle to two short straps at the base of the knapsack.[187]

Although issued to most of the Peninsular troops mobilised for war, the knapsack was too uncomfortable for general campaign duty in the subtropical climate of Cuba and the other colonies. Like his American counterpart, the Spanish soldier of 1898 usually felt more comfortable carrying a blanket roll. Provisions were also sometimes carried in a white cotton haversack attached to a shoulder sling of the same material. Water bottles, or *bota para vino*, were made of leather and carried two quarts, with a mouthpiece of horn or box wood.

Above, top right, right.

Flag details: the 30th Alfonso XIII Rifle Battalion; the 3rd Principe Infantry Regiment, commanded by Lieutenant Colonel Jose Patino Rodriguez, served in the Santiago de Cuba Division; the 1st Valladolid Infantry Battalion. Ben K. Weed Collection/Madison, Wisconsin, Capitol Flag Museum.

Bottom.

Flag of the 1st Battalion, 15th Extremadura Infantry Regiment. This unit served with the Spanish Light Division in Cuba during 1898, and was commanded by Lieutenant Colonel Eloy Hervas Martinez. The regimental motto underneath the device on the faded yellow bar means 'The Scaler'. Ben K. Weed Collection.

Each regiment and battalion had a flag which was carried by the officer of the staff, or *Alférez Abandero*, specially detailed for the duty. Although silk embroidered flags were prescribed for parade and ceremonial occasions, those borne in battle by 1898 were generally made of cotton bunting. Composed of a tricolor in red and yellow Spanish national colours, flags of line infantry regiments and battalions were embellished with a black-painted crown over the royal coat of arms and regimental designation, all facing towards the fly end of the central yellow bar. Rifle, or *cazadore*, battalions bore a black-painted crown over a bugle horn and unit designation, facing in the same direction. Dimensions of flags seem to have varied. That carried by the 30th Alfonso XIII Rifle Battalion was almost square, measuring 33 inches on the staff by 33½ inches on the fly. When furled, flags were carried in an oilskin sheath lined with white linen.

Since 15 November 1879, each company within a line infantry regiment had carried a guidon, or *banderine*, of a distinctive colour with either an embroidered or painted company number, for example, 1st Company – red; 2nd Company – yellow; 3rd Company – white; 4th Company – green. If there were more than four companies in a battalion, they were distinguished as follows: 5th Company – violet; 6th Company – light blue; 7th Company – red and white; 8th Company – yellow and green.[188.] These were originally to be made of merino wool or fine flannel, and measured 28 centimetres on the staff by 40 centimetres on the fly. A guidon surviving in the collection of the *Museo de la Ciudad* in Cuba does not conform to this colour scheme. Composed of a national flag with '8A' in its centre in red lace, it has a branch of laurel leaves on either side.

Colonial units carried various types of flags. Although re-designated the 70th regiment of the line by 1898, the 3rd Magallanes Infantry Regiment, a native Filipino unit commanded by Spanish officers, carried a national banner with crown and royal coat of arms in full colour, and facing towards the bottom edge of the field, surrounded by the inscription 'Regimiento de Yfanteria Magallanes, Nº. 3' in black capital letters. This flag is preserved today in the *Museo de Arte Oriental de Valladolid*.[189] A small dark blue, triangular pennon once carried by a volunteer rifle battalion in Cuba also survives in the *Museo de la Ciudad* collection. Bearing the designation '1º Bat. 2n Cia. Cuerpo de Voluntarios de Matanzas' in silver letters along all of its three outer edges, it has a silver bugle horn in its centre. It is still attached to the original staff topped by a lance-tip and cross bar.[190]

Spanish Regular Army, General officers and staff

Subsequent to the Constitutional Law of 19 July 1889, general officers of the Spanish Army wore for full, or *gala*, dress a single-breasted tunic of deep blue, or *azul turqui*, fastened by nine gilt, convex buttons bearing in relief a crown and sunburst set within a wreath, above which was a Roman sword crossed with a baton. The red, low-standing collar was embellished with rich gold oakleaf embroidery; the round red cuffs, or *bocamangas*, were edged with gold lace and trimmed with bands of gold oakleaf embroidery – three for Captain General, two for Lieutenant General, and one for General of Division. Brigadier generals' cuffs were also edged with gold but bore one band of silver oakleaf embroidery. The rank of general was also distinguished by epaulettes with gold lace straps and gold bullion fringe, a crimson waist sash, or *faja*, with gold tassels, and a red shoulder sash, or *fajin*. Trousers were also deep blue with broad gold lace seam stripes which matched that worn on the coat. Full dress headgear consisted of a black patent leather helmet with a gilt plate bearing the Royal Coat of Arms and white feather plume.[191]

The daily uniform for general officers since 1886 had consisted of a deep blue single-breasted coat with two breast pockets, gold shoulder cords, and cuff insignia the same as per full dress, red sash and madder red trousers with two medium-width dark blue seam stripes. Headgear consisted of a white felt *Leopoldina*-pattern cap with black patent leather top, visor and strap. This was trimmed around the top with gold lace and around the bottom with a dark blue band of cloth embellished with rich oak-leaf embroidery. At the front was the national cockade of red and yellow, over which was a gold lace loop, secured by a gilt general officers' button. This was surmounted by a gilt metal acorn. Dark blue cloth caps of the *Teresiana*-pattern, complete with oak-leaf embroidered band, were worn for undress.

A white drill version of the coat worn for undress, but with a falling collar, was worn on campaign by general officers of the Colonial Army. Detachable cuff rank insignia was also the same as for full dress and undress, with gold cord shoulder straps. Trousers were plain white drill. A soft wide-topped campaign cap worn by Brigadier General Joaquin Vara de Rey, who fell commanding the Spanish defence at El Caney, survives in the collection of the *Museo del Ejército*. Made from off-white cloth with a fine cord weave, it bears a single band of silver oakleaf embroidery on a dark blue base, and has a patent leather visor and chin strap.

The uniform of the officers of the general staff followed, in style and ornamentation, that worn by infantry officers of the line, but their branch service colour was light blue, as were their silk sashes. Buttons bore a crown above a five-pointed star, encircled by a wreath, around which was a scroll bearing the designation 'Cuerpo de. E. M. del Ejercito', or Corps of the General Staff of the Army. An aiguillette of twisted gold cord was worn suspended from the right shoulder. Trousers were deep blue with two broad, light blue seam stripes. Full dress headgear consisted of a white felt *Leopoldina* cap topped with a light blue feather plume.

Spanish Regular Army, Infantry and Rifles

The Spanish Infantry of the Line consisted of 74 regiments, each of two battalions, while the Rifles, or *Cazadores*, amounted to at least 30 battalions. Spanish infantry regiments and rifle battalions were designated by a territorial appellation and a consecutive number, thus *Regimiento de Castilla, No. 16*, or *Battallon de Cazadores de Barcelona, No. 7*. The Colonial Army possessed the following units: 56 line battalions and ten rifle companies in Cuba; one regiment of infantry

Spanish officers resplendent in full dress. (left) Valeriano Weyler y Nicolau, Captain-General of Cuba (1896–1897), dubbed the 'Butcher' by the American press because of his ruthless reign of repression in Cuba. (right) General Borbon y Castellvi, second uncle of King Alfonso XIII, imprisoned in the fortress of Santona, near Santander, for shouting 'Viva España' when the American flag was hauled down at the Embassy in Madrid in 1898! They wear deep blue coats with red collar richly embroidered with oak-leaf pattern, and proudly display an array of medals and military crosses. From 'Photographic History of the Spanish-American War' (1898).

and two rifle battalions, plus 14 volunteer battalions, in Puerto Rico; seven regiments of infantry and 15 rifle battalions in the Philippines. These units were similarly designated *Regimiento Infanteria de la Habana, No. 66* and *Battallon de Cazadores de la Regimiento Expedicionario, No. 1.*

The staff of an infantry regiment consisted of one colonel, one bandmaster, one bugler major and 36 musicians. A regiment contained two battalions, each made up of four active, or service, companies and one depot or recruiting company. Each battalion was under one lieutenant colonel, two majors (one in charge of internal economy, styled *Jefe del Detail*) and the other temporarily acting as Paymaster; one captain

adjutant, one captain quartermaster, one ensign who carried the colours, one chaplain, one officer of the Medical Department, one master armourer and one bugler (either a sergeant of corporal). On paper, a peacetime infantry company contained one captain, two lieutenants, two ensigns (one of them supernumerary), one sergeant major, three sergeants, five corporals, five lance corporals, two buglers, one cadet, four 1st class privates and 178 2nd class privates in peacetime. In wartime the latter was increased to 228 men. In practise, most colonial companies in Cuba and the Philippines were constantly reduced to half strength due to disease or battle casualties.

The Rifles were considered to be the 'Corps d'Elite' of the Spanish Infantry. The staff of a Rifle Battalion was, with the addition of a bandmaster and 27 musicians, the same as that of a line battalion. A battalion of Rifles consisted of four service companies and a depot company. A rifle company had one bugler more and two privates less than an ordinary infantry company.

Peninsular Dress

Originally adopted for daily wear by the infantry in November 1884, and officially prescribed for general dress in 1886, the single-breasted jacket, or *guerrera*, of deep-blue flannel had a low standing collar which bore either side the number of the regiment in gilt numerals. Those worn by officers were fastened by seven gilt, convex buttons, bearing in relief the royal arms of Spain, with the pillars of Hercules either side, below which was a scroll displaying the word 'Infanteria'. Parallel with the third button were two 13 centimetre-long breast pockets with flaps. Officers' jackets were edged with black mohair, and the rear skirts possessed two false pockets, with six large buttons sewn in pairs – two at the top, two in the centre, and two at the bottom of the openings. A six centimetre-long opening either side at the waist permitted the wearer to carry a revolver and sword attached to the waist belt underneath.[192]

Rifle Battalions wore the same pattern of jacket, except that the collar bore a metal bugle horn device with the unit number inset, while on the sleeves three special pieces of pointed braid called *sardinetas* were sewn just above the top seam of each cuff, thus indicating the élite status of the corps. These were gold lace, edged with black thread, and measured three centimetres square. Reserve and Depot battalions of both infantry and rifles wore on the collar an 'R' or 'D', respectively, in gilt metal letters, over which was a small gilt plate bearing the regimental number.

Officers of the field and staff of both infantry and rifles were distinguished as follows: cuffs were edged with 6 millimetre-wide gold lace bullion, or *galones*, of five strands, and decorated with a series of eight-ray stars embroidered from 'dull' gold twist, measuring 30 millimetres in diameter. As per Royal Order of 19 July 1889, this consisted of three bands of lace and three stars for a colonel; two each of the same for a lieutenant colonel; one gold and one silver band of lace, one gold and one silver star, for a 1st commandant; two gold lace bands and two gold stars for a 2nd commandant.

Company grade officers' cuffs were edged with gold braid, or *trencillas*, of five strands, the same width as for field and staff, above which a series of embroidered six-pointed stars measuring 25 millimetres in diameter were sewn to the coat sleeve. A captain wore three bands of braid above which were three stars; a first lieutenant, two bands of braid and two stars; a second lieutenant, since 6 August 1890, two bands of braid and two stars – the outer braid of gold and the inner of silver, and the inner star of silver and outer one of gold. Shoulder straps for all field and company grade officers consisted of a gold lace cord secured near the collar by a small regulation button

Spanish Troops in Cuba, 1898.

In this street scene in Havana, a Marine Infantry sergeant stood at left is dressed in the all-white cotton drill uniform issued to his unit on colonial service. He is armed with a Spanish Model 1893 Mauser rifle. The officer of the Hussars of Havana, a prestigious volunteer unit which formed the guard at the Palace of the Captain General, wears his full dress uniform while on Palace duty. A member of the Civil Guard is stood in the rear in service uniform with detachable red collar and cuff facings, and distinctive purple-lined cape draped over his shoulder. He holds a Model 1871 Remington 'Rolling Block' rifle. The Private, First Class, of the 13th Merida Rifle Battalion, wears his *rayadillo* campaign uniform with detachable green facings on collar and cuffs. His rank is distinguished by the long inverted chevron worn on his left arm only. Painting by Richard Hook.

and sewn to the coat at the shoulder seam.

For full dress occasions, officers wore around their necks a brass gorget bearing in silver the royal crown over the numerals 'XIII' superimposed on the letter 'A' indicating Adolphus XIII. This was suspended from a gold cord attached by two small decorated gilt metal buttons. Infantry officers wore a belt of black patent leather measuring four centimetres wide, fastened by a gilt metal loop and clasp buckle bearing in silver the Arms of Spain above which was the Royal Crown.

According to the Royal Order of 5 September 1884, infantry officers wore a great-coat, or *capote*, of deep blue on campaign duty in Europe. This garment was made to fit loose, with skirts which fell to 20 centimetres below the knee for field grade officers, and 11 centimetres for company grade officers. A low-standing collar of velvet, of the same colour as the coat, was fastened with hooks and eyes underneath the chin. The sleeves were 16 centimetres wide at the wrist, with 8.8 centimetre deep cuffs, bearing one small button sewn just above the cuff. Shoulder wings were red for infantry regiments, reserve and depot battalions, and green for rifle battalions, and were edged with 15 millimetre-thick twisted trim, or *tornillo* thread. These were secured to the shoulder by a small button sewn two centimetres away from the seam of the collar.

The double-breasted front of the great-coat was fastened with two rows of six buttons each, 22 centimetres apart with the top pair at shoulder height and the bottom pair level with the hips. In the left hip was a 15 centimetre-long opening for the hilt of the sword, in order that the wearer might draw his sword without removing his coat. In the back were two 17 centimetre-wide pockets, level with the bottom two

This Rifleman wears the campaign uniform of the Spanish Peninsular Army, which consisted of blue-grey *capote*, or greatcoat, with green shoulder wings and sleeve trim. His dark blue trousers have double seam stripes of green worsted braid. Note the *sardinetas* on his cuffs, which denote the élite status of his regiment, and his *alpartagas* or hempen sandals. His oil-skin covered *ros* stands on the studio prop to his right. Woollen uniforms like this were too warm for the climate in Cuba and the Philippines. From 'A Photographic History of the Spanish-American War' (1898).

front buttons, each being closed by five small buttons. The lining was of black silk.

Enlisted infantrymen wore a great-coat of greyish sky-blue cloth of the same basic cut and length as prescribed for company-grade officers. The collar was red and at each side bore the number of the regiment. The back and sleeves were lined with strong white cotton cloth. Shoulder straps were of the same colour as the coat, with red edging. Riflemen wore the same type of coat, but with collar and shoulder strap trim of emerald green, the former bearing the bugle horn within which was the number of the unit. *Sardinetas* decorated the cuffs.

Infantry trousers were of madder red cloth, and since 15 November 1884 had been trimmed with a double seam stripe of indigo blue, each stripe being 22 millimetres wide with a 6 millimetres gap between. In 1893, the Rifles received indigo, or dark blue, trousers with double green seam stripes, of the same pattern as for infantry. These often appear to have faded to light or sky blue in the field. When mounted, infantry officers wore long leggings, or *polaina*, of black calf skin. Leggings of the same material were issued to enlisted men on campaign duty. Gloves were of white 'Scottish cotton', beaver, or buckskin for officers and white cotton for other ranks.

Full dress headgear for officers consisted of a grey felt cap, or *ros*, with gold lace around the top – three strands for a colonel, and two for other field officers – and black patent leather top, strap and visor. The national cockade of muslin, with gold lace loop and button, was attached to the front, and was surmounted by a scarlet pompon for full dress and a gilt metal grenade for daily wear. Rifle Battalions wore a green pompon, while field officers and adjutants, music majors and cornet sergeants were distinguished by a white pompon. For daily wear, officers wore a *Teresiana* cap of blue cloth with gold lace trim around the top and band. At the front of this was attached a three centimetre-diameter national cockade, over which was superimposed a gold loop of six ribs and one small button. The visor and chin strap were of patent leather.

The rank and file wore the same type of jacket as officers, of deep blue flannel with plain low standing collar, shoulder straps and cuffs. Fastened by seven gilt buttons bearing the number of the regiment, inset in a bugle horn for Rifles, this garment had two breast pockets with flaps and six buttons, three either side, on the rear skirts. Rank insignia for NCOs consisted of a series of diagonal bars on the lower fore-arm of both coat sleeves: two yellow cloth bars for 1st sergeant; one yellow bar for 2nd sergeant; three red worsted bars for 1st corporal; two red bars for 2nd corporal. A First Class soldier was distinguished by a long, inverted, red worsted chevron on the left sleeve extending from the shoulder to the elbow.

Headgear for enlisted men was a grey felt *ros*, with either red or green ribbed lace around the top seam, dependent on whether the unit was line infantry or rifles. At the front of this was the national cockade with worsted cord loop and button. Pompons and gilt grenades corresponded to those worn by officers. A black oilskin cover, with detachable neck flap of the same material, was worn in wet weather, or when otherwise authorised. In the summer, a white cotton 'havelock' was permitted.

Every day headgear for enlisted men also consisted

These Spanish officers probably belong to the 16th Castilla Infantry Regiment, which served in Cuba. The colonel is seated fourth from the left in the second row from the front. They wear their service dress uniform of deep blue jackets and madder red pants, and have waterproof covers over their *Leopoldina*-pattern caps. Note that breast pocket flaps appear to be optional. The only named individual in this group is Captain Gabril Gomado Cilcuin, who stands fifth from the right at the back. The officer stood at ground level second from right wears a gorget around his neck. Museo del Ejército, Madrid.

of a barracks cap similar to the pill box cap worn by the British Army of the day. Adopted in 1886, it was made of dark blue cloth, lined with sheepskin for officers, with branch service trim. It bore a worsted tassel and number of the regiment, embroidered in the same colour. Those worn by rifle battalions carried a bugle horn with the unit number inset.

Colonial Dress

The everyday uniform for infantry officers in the Colonial Army during the 1890s consisted of a white drill blouse with falling collar, patterned after the blue jacket, and plain white drill trousers. Regimental designation was indicated by gilt numerals fastened either side of the collar. Detachable collar and cuff-facings, red for infantry and green for rifles, and bearing appropriate rank insignia, were worn for parade and inspection. These could be removed for campaign duty. Cuff rank insignia was the same as for general service, with gold cord shoulder straps for field and staff officers, while plain white cloth shoulder straps appear to have been worn by company grade officers. Headgear consisted of a straw hat with national cockade, the latter officially only worn for parade or on ceremonial occasions.

Photographic evidence suggests that enlisted men in some colonial regiments were also issued with white service uniforms, of the same pattern as the *guerrera*, with plain standing collar and shoulder straps. Caps of the *Teresiana*-pattern, with white tops, were also worn.

For campaign dress, officers and enlisted infantrymen in the Colonial Army wore a jacket and trousers of *rayadillo*, after the same pattern as the white drill blouse, with detachable collar and cuff-facings. Rank insignia for NCOs was the same as for everyday wear, but appears to have been only loosely attached to the sleeve for easy removal when washing the uniform. Headgear was usually the *jipijapa*, but visorless barracks caps of *rayadillo* were also often worn.

Company flag, or *banderin*, of the 8th company of a Spanish infantry unit in the Philippines. Company flags were usually reserved for ceremonial occasions, and were not carried on campaign. This silk version was returned to Spain by D. Carlos Pascuel del Pobil and Martinez de Medinillo who served as volunteers in the unit. Museo del Ejército, Madrid.

The *rayadillo* uniform of the Rifle Battalions was basically the same as for infantry, although their élite status was indicated by three yellow braid *sardineta* attached to each cuff, and a gilt metal bugle-horn insignia, with the number of the regiment in the centre, secured to either side of the collar. One

Caps worn by Spanish generals. (left) A *Leopoldina* cap with stiffened white felt body and gilt metal acorn. (right) A *Teresiana cap* with soft body. Note the rich oak-leaf embroidery on both. Museo del Ejército, Madrid.

surviving pair of rifleman's *rayadillo* trousers has one-inch wide green seam stripes, which were presumably not removable. [193]

Artillery

As a result of the Royal Orders of 29 July and 16 December 1891, and a further reorganisation dated 29 August 1893, the artillery corps of the Spanish Peninsular Army consisted of the following units: 14 mounted, or field, artillery regiments, each of eight batteries of six guns, of either 8 or 9-centimetre calibre, with an equal number of artillery ammunition columns, totalling 25,606 men; two mountain artillery regiments, each with four batteries of 8-centimetre guns, plus ammunition columns, amounting to 7,254 men; ten battalions of fortress artillery, partly of six, and partly of four, companies each, totalling 8,175 men. Also in reserve were a further seven field artillery regiments with 136 guns served by 14,140 men.[194]

In Cuba, the Colonial Army artillery consisted of two regiments of mountain artillery and two battalions of fortress artillery. Only one battalion of fortress artillery was stationed on Puerto Rico, whilst the Philippines contained one regiment of mountain artillery and one of fortress artillery.

A regiment of fortress artillery was composed of two battalions of four companies, and in theory contained a total of 32 subalterns, 24 sergeants and 800 gunners. The regimental staff comprised a colonel, one bandmaster, one band-sergeant and 36 musicians. A battalion was commanded by a lieutenant

colonel, who was supported by one commandant, two captains (one an adjutant and paymaster), one ensign, one chaplain, one surgeon, one trumpeter and one armourer. In war time, a full-strength company was composed of one captain, two lieutenants, two sub-lieutenants, six sergeants, 14 corporals, three trumpeters, 12 1st class gunners and 215 2nd class gunners.

The staff of a regiment of mountain artillery was the same as above. Each regiment consisted of six batteries, composed of four guns, four horses and 30 mules. The personnel of each battery comprised one captain, three lieutenants, one veterinary surgeon, one sergeant major, two sergeants, two trumpeters, 13 corporals, three farriers, three artificers and 92 gunners.[195]

Regarding full dress, horse artillery batteries were required via the Royal Order of 2 July 1890 to wear a double-breasted tunic, or *guerrera-levita*, of deep blue cloth with two rows of seven gilt metal buttons bearing a crown above two crossed cannon and pyramid of balls, set against a dark blue enamelled background. The collar was scarlet with blue edging, while the front and bottom edges of the garment were trimmed with scarlet piping. The cuffs were embellished with a broad band of scarlet braid forming an inverted chevron. Shoulder straps, or wings, were of dark blue cloth with scarlet trim and pad. The rear skirts contained two pockets edged with scarlet, with one button at the hip, and one at the end of each pocket. A gilt metal 'flaming bomb' insignia was attached either side of the collar. On 28 November 1890, this tunic was prescribed for all other branches of the Corps of Artillery in the Spanish Army.[196]

Since 1891, artillery officers had also worn a short, blue coat with black beaver fur collar, and black astrakhan and goat hair trimming around the front and bottom edges, fastened in front with three black lace knots and wooden toggles.

A white felt *Teresiana* had a gold *forrajera*, or worsted cord, worn around the neck and attached to the back of the cap. This headgear bore the artillery cap plate above which was the national cockade, with gold lace fastener, having in its centre a small artillery button of 'flaming bomb' pattern. Belts and accoutrements were of white leather. Trousers were deep blue with broad red seam stripes, and footwear consisted of black leather half-boots. Grey cotton, or chamois, gloves were worn with the everyday uniform, while white cotton ones were reserved for full dress.

Daily dress for artillery officers of foot and mountain artillery consisted a deep-blue seven-button short jacket, or *guerrera*, edged with dark blue braid,

with two flapless breast pockets, gold shoulder cords and eight-inch side vents either side of the skirt. Caps were dark blue of the *Teresiana*-pattern trimmed with gold braid. A blue flannel barracks cap was usually worn with undress.

Enlisted men wore a seven-button *guerrera* of deep-blue flannel, with red worsted epaulettes, and facing colour and 'flaming bomb' insignia the same as for officers. Buttons worn by cannoneers displayed the word 'Bombero' on a plain polished background. Headgear was the same as for officers.

Artillery Colonial Campaign Dress

In the tropics, the Colonial artillery wore either white drill, or *rayadillo*, uniforms with detachable dark blue facings on the collar and cuffs. An artillery uniform

An unused card of Spanish 3rd rifle regiment buttons produced by Trelon, Weldon & Weil, of Paris. The letters 'T. W. & W.' may just be seen in the brand mark printed on the remains of the wrapping paper. They were captured from the Havana Arsenal by the U.S. Army in 1898. Many were sold as U.S. Government surplus to the Bannerman Arms Company of New York, which featured them in their catalogues for many years. Ben K. Weed Collection.

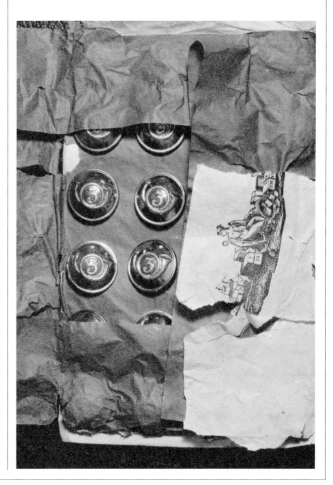

These officers belonged to either the 24th Alfonso XIII Rifle Battalion, or the 25th Patria Rifle Battalion, both of which were stationed in Puerto Rico before the American invasion. Their Rifle status is indicated by the bugle horn insignia on their collars and *sardinetas* on their detachable green cuffs. Two men in the back row wear sun helmets, one of which has a neck flap. Ben K. Weed Collection.

preserved in the collection of the *Museo de la Revolucion* in Havana has a jacket with very dark blue cuffs and a ring of gold braid, a brass 'flaming bomb' on the collar ends, and a gold lace shoulder cord. Trousers of the same cloth have dark blue seam stripes. The accompanying *jipijapa* hat has a black band, but is minus the national cockade.[197]

Cavalry

There were 28 cavalry regiments of four squadrons, each containing 596 horses and 700 men, in the Spanish Peninsular Army. This was supplemented by 14 reserve regiments. Regarding the Colonial forces, the Army of Cuba contained 10 cavalry regiments, while only one native cavalry regiment, plus a volunteer squadron, formed part of the Army of the Philippines.

The field and staff of a cavalry regiment consisted of one colonel, one lieutenant colonel, three commandants, four captains, four adjutants, one lieutenant (paymaster), one chaplain, one surgeon, one 1st-class veterinary surgeon, one 2nd-class veterinary surgeon, two 3rd-class veterinary surgeons, one riding-master, one saddle-maker, one armourer, one trumpet-major and one corporal-trumpeter. A squadron was composed of one captain, three lieutenants, two sub-lieutenants, one sergeant-major, four sergeants, eight 1st-class corporals, eight 2nd-class corporals, four trumpeters, three farriers, one smith, four 1st-class troopers and 91 troopers.

A lancer regiment consisted of three squadrons armed with the lance and sword, and a fourth, called the 'dragoon squadron', carried the Mauser carbine and sword. Hussars, dragoons, mounted rifles and detached squadrons were armed in the same manner as the fourth squadron of lancers.

Since 11 June 1892, Spanish lancer, dragoon, and mounted rifle regiments had worn sky-blue jackets, or *guerreras*, with a double row of silver buttons and trimmed with white braid on the collar and cuffs. Belts were of 'nutbrown' leather. Trousers for all before 1894 had been of madder red with a double seam stripe of sky blue, but during July of that year they

Spanish soldiers returning from Cuba receive hospitality from the ladies of Cadiz. The ensign, or *alférez,* at right wears a *Teresiana*-style cap with his undress uniform. The three enlisted men at left wear dark blue flannel barracks caps with their service jackets. Note the officer in full dress grey felt *Leopoldina* cap standing behind the table. From 'A Photographic History of the Spanish-American War' (1898).

were officially changed to sky blue with a double seam stripe of white. The latter change was slow, and as late as 1896, the Dragoons still wore their red trousers.[198]

Regarding full dress headgear, the Lancers wore helmets with brass mounts and spikes, similar to those worn by British heavy cavalry, and adorned with white plumes. The Mounted Rifles wore a sky-blue cap, with black visor and 'havelock', and band of white braid around the top. Until March 1895, the Dragoons possessed the same helmet as the Lancers, but in this year they adopted the Mounted Rifles-pattern shako.

Spanish Hussar regiments continued to wear very colourful full dress uniforms. The Princesa Hussars wore a white shako with yellow braid, a sky blue dolman with yellow trim on the cuffs, and nine rows of yellow Brandenburg braid on the chest. The pelisse was white with black fur and trim. The Pavia Hussars had a similar uniform, but the shako and dolman were madder red, while their pelisse was sky-blue. Both regiments wore sky-blue trousers with double yellow seam stripes.

For everyday duty, officers wore a sky-blue *Teresiana*-pattern cap with white braid for lancers, mounted rifles and dragoons, and yellow for the Princesa Hussars. That worn by the Pavia Hussars was madder red with yellow braid. In November 1894 the lancers, dragoons and mounted rifles received the new sky blue round barracks cap with two white bands, one on the central seam and the other around the top. The cap worn by the Princesa Hussars was sky-blue with yellow trim, while that of the Pavia Hussars was madder red trimmed yellow.[199]

During 1894, cavalry regiments of the line were authorised, for drill and home active service, a blue *guerrera*-style jacket with madder red collar and edging, fastened by a single row of seven buttons, and bearing the number of the regiment in silver numerals on the collar. Officers' rank was indicated via the same system as used by the other branches of service. Trousers were of deep blue denim with broad madder red seam stripes. Head dress consisted of a white felt *Leopoldina* cap, and black patent leather top, visor and chin strap. The national cockade was fastened by a silver loop, with a small silver button in the centre.

Mid-length patent leather boots were worn for ceremonial occasions.[200]

On campaign in the Colonies, Spanish cavalry wore either white drill, or *rayadillo*, campaign uniforms minus special insignia, with detachable red facings on the collar and cuffs. Possibly for everyday wear, officers wore a *Teresiana* cap, although the ubiquitous *jipijapa* was more practical.

Engineers

The Royal Corps of Engineers in the Peninsular Army consisted of four sapper and miner regiments of 2,000 men each; one mounted pontoon regiment of 3,442 men; one railway regiment of 1,040 men; and one telegraph battalion of 1,272 men.[201] A regiment of sappers and miners was composed of two battalions, the first three companies in each battalion being Sappers and the fourth company Miners. The first battalion of the Pontoon Regiment were Pontoniers, and the second battalion possessed two troops of Telegraphers and two of Railway Artificers.

The Army of Cuba contained the First Battalions of the 3rd and 4th Regiments of Sappers and Miners, a railway battalion, and a telegraph battalion. One telegraph company was present on Puerto Rico, and one battalion of sappers and miners in the Philippines.

Each company of engineers consisted of one captain, three lieutenants, one sergeant major, six sergeants, six 1st class corporals, six 2nd class corporals, four buglers, eight artificers, eight 1st class privates and 91 2nd class privates. Having the same basic composition, a mounted engineer troop had eight 1st class corporals, eight 2nd class corporals, four trumpeters, plus one farrier and one smith.

When placed on a war footing, the Pontoon Regiment had 15 wagons, each of which was equipped to carry a section of regulation bridge, composed of seven pontoons plus the *matériel* necessary for a bridge of 57 metres. In addition, they carried the Terrer mountain bridge suitable for a span of 17 metres. The Telegraph and Railway troops had at their disposal 34 mules for transport purposes.[202]

Since November 1890, officers of the Engineers had worn a service uniform consisting of a *guerrera*-style jacket with two rows of seven convex buttons, and shoulder straps of silver cord. Engineer soldiers wore a single-breasted jacket with red facings on the collar and cuffs, and edges trimmed with red braid. Also adopted in 1890 was a fur-trimmed overcoat, and sabre with steel scabbard. Sappers and Miners were distinguished by a cap plate and buttons bearing a crossed mattocks device, heads up, with a spade perpendicular between them. Buttons worn by the Pontoniers bore a crown above the Spanish arms in an oval shield, with the letters 'I'(for *Ingenieros*) and 'P' in script either side. Telegraphers wore gilt buttons bearing a crown above thunderbolts, tied in the centre with a bowknot, encircled by the appellation *Cuerpo de Telegrafos*. Railways troops had gilt buttons displaying a six-wheel locomotive.[203]

In 1893, the Engineer officers were permitted to wear for fatigue a short greyish sky-blue cape, service jacket and blouse. On campaign in the Colonies, Engineer officers and men wore red collar and cuff facings on their white drill and *rayadillo* uniforms.

Military Health

The climate, tropical disease, the *machete* and *mambí* bullets kept the Corps of Military Health, or *Sanidad Militar*, of the Spanish Army very busy during the conflict of 1898. Doctors toiled in hospitals filled with sick or wounded soldiers, or accompanied marching columns through the swamp, with mules loaded with medicine and instruments. Mules used by the *Sanidad Militar* were rigged in the same manner as per Mountain Artillery, but carried two beech wood medicine chests painted grey with black ironwork, a stretcher and small cask for water. The maximum weight carried by the average mule amounted to approximately eight *arrobas* of 25lbs each.

Doctor's assistants were ordinary soldiers trained as medical orderlies or stretcher bearers. They worked in teams of two carrying the wounded on stretchers made from two poles with a canvas bed stretched across. Medicines and instruments were also carried by Military Health personnel in a knapsack bearing the letters 'S M'.

The Director of Military Medical Service in Cuba in 1898 was Subinspector, Physician 1st Class, Cristobel Mas y Bonnebal, who was responsible for ten military hospitals on the island. Officers of Military Health wore the same full dress, daily dress and campaign uniform as the branch of service to which they were attached, although their gilt buttons bore the letter 'S' superimposed on the letter 'M'.

Civil Guard

The Civil Guard was the crack force of the Spanish Army. Composed of eight *tercios*, or regiments, of 750 men each on the Peninsula, membership required literacy and good physical health. The Civil Guard in Cuba consisted of 1,700 dismounted men from the 17th, 18th and 19th Regiments, and a cavalry

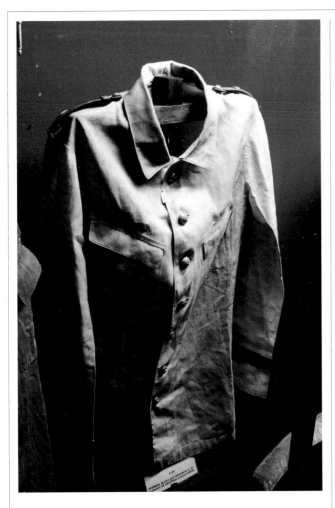

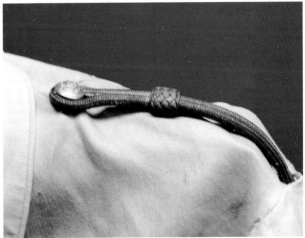

Above.
White tropical jacket worn by Lieutenant Colonel Julián Fortea Selvi, Military Governor of the Isle of Batanes in the Philippines.

Top right.
Cuff insignia, including two eight-pointed stars, indicating the rank of lieutenant colonel.

Right.
Detail showing gold braid shoulder strap. Museo del Ejército, Madrid.

regiment composed of two squadrons, commanded by Colonel Guillermo Tort y Gil. This force was supplemented by a volunteer squadron of 125 men. The 20th Regiment was posted in the Philippines, while a further mixed unit of both mounted and infantry garrisoned Puerto Rico.

The general duties of the Civil Guard included ensuring that both military and civil orders were duly executed. They were also expected to be familiar with the topography of the country, especially regarding roads and means of communication. They had considerable autonomous responsibility, should sedition or revolution break out in the Colonies. In

time of war, their post was expected to be at the front, but during the investment of Santiago de Cuba in 1898, only one section of the Civil Guard was stationed in the vicinity. Their principal duties during this period included riot control and the prevention of looting, while a few men manned the guns of the Socapa battery in Santiago harbour. However, during the entire Cuban revolution and the war of 1898, the Civil Guard served with general bravery, a total of 1,460 members being killed and 3,082 wounded.

The uniform of the Civil Guard on the Peninsula was of a heavy dark blue wool consisting of a double-

This image of two Spanish officers was captured by English photographer 'Señor Roque', whose studio was situated at 'No. 10, corner of calle de Carriedo' in Manila. Wearing their white tropical uniforms, the man seated displays the cuff insignia of a captain, whilst a lieutenant is stood by his side. Note the 'hunting horn' insignia on their collars, denoting their Rifle Regiment status. Their sword belts are worn under their coats, with the sword straps threaded through openings in the waist of their coats. Museo del Ejército, Madrid.

This First Corporal wears a neat white drill jacket with his madder red trousers. His white-topped *Teresiana*-style cap bears the numerals '74' on a coloured band, which indicates that he was a member of the 74th Regiment of the Line, which was stationed at Cavite, near Manila, in the Philippines. Note that his three cuff bars were sewn to the sleeve at the ends only, leaving the remainder loose. The backmark on this image indicates that it was taken at the 'Antigua Photography' studio of 'Von Camp, 37 Escolta, Manila'. Museo del Ejército, Madrid.

breasted frock coat with red facings on standing collar and cuffs, twisted cord shoulder knots, yellow buckskin shoulder straps and belts, and a distinctive cocked hat of black patent leather. Proving unsuitable for general wear in the tropics, this uniform was reserved for formal inspections or reviews.

In Cuba, Civil Guard officers wore a full dress uniform composed of a dark blue seven-button jacket, or *guerrera*, with red facings on falling collar, and red cuffs displaying the rank system as worn by the regular army. One small button was also attached to each cuff, while four more were sewn on the rear skirts, either end of two concealed pockets; two were also placed as belt supports and the other two about six inches lower. Shoulder knots were silver. A jacket of the same cut, with two flapped breast pockets, but made from a

blue-grey linen, was worn by officers on campaign duty. This could also be faced red with silver shoulder knots. Trousers of the same colour had wide red seam stripes. Also worn by all ranks was a caped overcoat, or *capote*, of black cloth with purple lining.

Enlisted men wore the same pattern of uniform but, dependent on availability, the cloth used included blue-grey linen, dark khaki, and the ubiquitous *rayadillo*. In all cases, the falling collar and detachable cuffs were faced with red cloth, and had simple silver cord shoulder knots. Chevrons for NCOs were also of red cloth.

Headgear for all ranks in Cuba consisted of a soft grey felt, round hat with silk tape around the brim, looped up on left side from a small national cockade to a small button on the crown. Civil Guard units based

The men stood in front of Fort Paez, a small block house near Santa Clara, in Cuba, wear the typical colonial campaign dress of Spanish infantry. The officer third from left is resplendent in his white drill suit with detachable coloured cuff facings. The men probably wear *rayadillo*. Note the stripes on the NCO's forearms (third from right), and the guard with blanket roll stood by the doorway. Several men appear to have cockades pinned on the right hand side of the crown of their *jipijapas*.

From 'A Photographic History of the Spanish-American War' (1898).

in Puerto Rico and the Philippines seem to have favoured the sun helmet. Long boots were worn for mounted duty.[204]

Volunteers

Numerous Volunteer Battalions were formed in Cuba to re-inforce the Spanish Army during the period 1868–1898. In time, virtually every able-bodied male residing in Cuba saw service in this auxiliary force of some 80,000 men. Volunteer battalions were trained and organised like Spanish Regular units. The Spanish government furnished them with arms, but they bought their own uniforms and equipment, which were frequently paid for by *abonaré* chits, redeemable at the war's end.[205]

The Hussars of Havana, a prestigious volunteer unit which formed the guard at the Palace of the Captain General of Cuba, wore a special full dress uniform. The light blue jacket worn by officers was cut in the Hussar-style, with madder red collar and cuffs, and three rows of nine gilt buttons connected by Brandenburgs of gold braid. The back of this garment was embellished along the two outer seams with gold lace which terminated at the top with a cloverleaf knot. The edges of the cuffs were trimmed in the same style. Shoulder straps of gold cord were fastened by one small gilt button near the collar seam. The collar was adorned on either side with a gilt 'bugle horn', in the loop of which was a numeral '1'. The front skirts contained two small slanting pockets edged with gold braid, and had side vents trimmed in the same style. The waist belt was composed of four connecting strands of cord, alternating in red and yellow, with red cord sword slings tipped with gold. Rank was indicated by a series of stars on, or above, the red cuff facings, dependent on field or company grade designation.

Their madder red trousers had double gold lace seam stripes. Headgear consisted of a light blue *Teresiana*-pattern cap which sloped from 15.5 centimetres high at the back to 7.5 at the front,

trimmed with madder red around the upper half, with a band of gold lace about two centimetres wide around the top seam. The visor was black patent leather, and the chin strap was gilt scaled. Attached to the front was a national cockade with gilt plate bearing the Royal Coat of Arms. Below this a gilt bugle horn with the numeral '1' inset. Fastened to the back of the cap was a gilt plate with two gold *cordones*, or aiguillettes, which terminated in a loop around the wearer's neck. This cap was surmounted by a white feather plume. The sabretache was of black leather.

Daily wear for officers consisted of a *guerrera*-style jacket of grey/blue thin flannel cloth, similar to that worn by officers of the Civil Guard. Cut as for full dress, it was adorned with the same number of buttons which were connected by black silk braid Brandenburgs. The shoulder straps were also of black silk braid. White drill trousers were tucked into black riding boots.

The jacket worn by all other ranks was of blue denim of the same cut as per officers, being embellished with black worsted Brandenburgs and shoulder straps. Collar and cuffs were faced with madder red, while trousers were of white drill, and boots were black. Headgear consisted of the same pattern cap as for officers, with madder red trim on the upper half and a red horsehair plume. For campaign duty, the unit wore a straw hat with same suit.[206]

In 1880 the Volunteers Corps of Cuba and Puerto Rico received new uniform regulations, which were repeated in 1892, and applicable through the entire period until the war with the United States. According to these regulations the full dress uniform of the different branches of service was as follows: Infantry and Rifles: a grey felt *Leopoldina*, dark blue jacket with green collar and braid, and madder red trousers with green seam stripes; Cavalry: white felt *Leopoldina* with gold lace trim for officers, and yellow for troopers, dark blue jacket with madder red collar and yellow braid, madder red trousers with double dark blue seam stripes; Artillery: white felt *Leopoldina*, dark blue jacket with madder red trim around collar and cuffs, flaming grenades on the collar, gilt buttons, and madder red trousers with blue seam stripes; Engineers: same as the artillery but with white trim on jacket, and a gilt metal castle on the collar.

In theory, Volunteer units wore three different uniforms: full dress, everyday white linen or *rayadillo* wear and a *rayadillo* campaign uniform. The cost of full dress probably reduced its use to the minimum, and most wore everyday or campaign dress.

For daily wear, all branches of service wore the straw hat and a suit of *rayadillo*, with buttons, *sardinetas* and insignia of rank the same as for Regular Army full dress. The collar, cuffs and trouser seam stripes on these uniforms were faced with the following branch service colours, which were removed for campaign duty:

Infantry and Rifles	Green
Cavalry	Red
Artillery	Dark Blue

An artillery officer's cap plate with crossed cannon and pyramid of cannon balls. Ben K. Weed Collection.

Engineers	Red
Chaplains	Purple

Several examples of *rayadillo* uniforms worn by Cuban volunteers survive today, two of them being preserved in the *Museo de la Ciudad* in Havana. That worn by Lieutenant de Bon, of the 7th Volunteer Rifle Battalion, has gold lace trefoil shoulder straps, and green collar and cuff facings on the jacket. On both

A cavalry trooper's *rayadillo* uniform complete with detachable red facings and First Class soldier's chevron on the left sleeve. The artillery belt plate has been wrongly placed with this uniform, which is preserved in a museum in Puerto Rico. Photo courtesy of David Spencer.

Spanish cannoneers, wearing blue undress jackets and madder red trousers with broad blue seam stripes, man a Krupp rapid-fire mountain gun. Note the side vent and six rear buttons in the coat skirt of the man seated at the gun. From 'A Photographic History of the Spanish-American War' (1898).

sides of the collar is a brass bugle horn with the numeral '7' set within the loop on a red cloth patch. The cuffs have a single strand of gold braid, although the two six-pointed stars on the sleeve above do not entirely follow 1885 regulations. Three gold lace *sardinetas* are secured just above the cuffs. The trousers bear green seam stripes.

The uniform of Ramon Herrera Sancibrian, Conde de la Montera, who commanded the 5th Volunteer Rifle Battalion sometime during the last quarter of the 19th century, was basically the same as above, with regulation cuff rank insignia and *sardinetas*. Also worn by Colonel Herrera Sancibrian was a dark blue barracks cap piped with bright green cord, with three bands of gold lace sewn around near its base.

A *rayadillo* uniform surviving in the West Point Museum Collection belonged to a First Class Private of the 13th Merida Rifle Battalion, which was attached to the Light Division garrisoned in Holguin Province in Cuba during 1898. It also has detachable green

collar and cuff facings, and green trouser seam stripes. The jacket is unusual in that the *sardinetas* are sewn on to the cuffs as opposed to being immediately above them, as was customary.

In 1892, the volunteer infantry of the Philippines were prescribed a dress uniform consisting of a sun

Opposite top.
The 6th Battalion of the 4th Mountain Artillery Regiment was part of the Santiago de Cuba Division, and hence saw considerable action during July 1898. The officers are seen here in their blue service uniforms, which proved too hot for regular tropical wear. Colonel Wenceslao Farres Xarlant stands second from the right. The bare-headed man at rear left wears the fur-trimmed blue top coat prescribed for artillery officers in 1891. From 'A Photographic History of the Spanish-American War' (1898).

Opposite below.
Spanish artillerymen in Cuba wearing campaign uniforms. Four men sport the *forrajera,* or worsted cord, of dark blue with one end around the neck and the other attached to the back of the hat. Also note the NCO's stripes on the sleeve of the soldier sat second from right, 'flaming bomb' insignia on the collars of some, and the artillery short sword in the belt of the man stood in the centre. Ben K. Weed Collection.

Above left.
Spanish cavalry swords. (right) Model 1860 Light Cavalry sword. (left) Model 1895 sword with 'orthopedic grip'. This weapon was decreed by a Royal Order of 8 July 1895, and was very possibly in use in Cuba and the Philippines by 1898.

Above right.
Detail showing manufacturer's stamp – 'Artilleria Fabrica de Toledo', indicating it was made at the Toledo Arsenal. Conrad Cairns Collection.

Left.
The uniform of Captain Santiago Ramón y Cajal. Note this earlier model of jacket is without breast pockets. According to the 1860 regulations, the rank of captain was indicated by three inverted chevrons and three stars, a first lieutenant by two chevrons and stars, and a second lieutenant, a single chevron and star. This system was replaced by cuff insignia in 1885. Museo del Ejército, Madrid.

helmet with white drill cover, and red plume attached to the right side; a white linen jacket, or *guerrera*, with seven gilt buttons and shoulder straps of gold cord for officers, and of red cloth for enlisted men; jacket collars and cuffs were also faced red; trousers were of plain white linen. For daily use and on campaign duty,

A Civil Guard officer's belt plate. Ben K. Weed Collection.

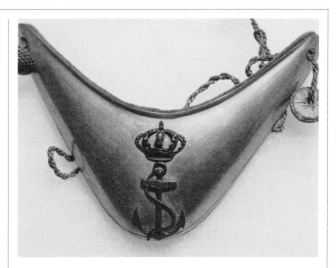

A gorget worn by a Spanish Marine Infantry officer. Ben K. Weed Collection.

a *rayadillo* jacket and trousers were worn with either straw hat, commonly turned up at the back, or the sun helmet, minus plume.[207]

Guerrillas

Spanish guerrilla units were composed of either paid mercenaries or volunteers whose officers were generally regular Army or Marine personnel. The task of the guerrillas was to seek out Cuban revolutionaries and sympathisers, and to punish them, usually with death! According to Major Enrique Ubieta Mauri, aide-de-camp to General Blanco, there were probably about 7,000 guerrillas attached to the Spanish Army when the war with the U.S. began. At least 1,000 were present in the vicinity of Santiago de Cuba when the Americans landed in 1898, and they took part in every major engagement and battle during the Cuban campaign.

Guerrillas were usually organised into companies or troops of between 60 to 100 men, and their uniforms generally followed the regulations of the Colonial army, with campaign dress of either *rayadillo*, white or brown drill. Weapons and accoutrements were supplied by Spain, and usually consisted of the M1871 Remington 'Rolling Block' rifle, or the machete.

Spanish Navy

According to Fred T. Jane, the Spanish Navy of 1898

Santiago Ramón y Cajal served in Cuba as an officer in the *Sanidad Militar*, and wears the sleeve insignia of a captain as prescribed until 1885 on the sleeves of his *rayadillo* fatigue uniform. Note he also wears a *chaleco*, or waist coat, of the same material. Museo del Ejército, Madrid.

was composed of 36 vessels. Of these, none were large modern iron clad battleships, monitors, or rams. Six were modern armoured cruisers; two were protected cruisers with medium armament; three were lightly armoured cruisers; three were old cruisers, or vessels with little or no protection; nine were ships of 'little fighting value'; and 13 were either torpedo depot ships, catchers or destroyers.[208]

The naval officers who commanded these vessels wore a full dress uniform consisting of a double-

This street scene taken outside 'La Mal Aguena' in Manila captures the moment when a Spanish mounted detachment, possibly *Escadron de Lanceros Expeditionario*, salutes with drawn swords, or machetes, a passing infantry unit. Note the guidon bearer, and neatly docked tails of the horses. The infantry appear to be wearing their deep blue *guerreras* with white barracks caps, whilst their officers wear lighter-coloured jackets. Museo del Ejército, Madrid.

breasted dark blue coatee with two rows of seven gilt, convex buttons bearing a crown over an upright, fouled anchor enclosed in an oval banded ring. The collar was low-standing with broad, red turned-back lapels. The collar, edges of the lapels, buttoned front

This Civil Guard officer, identified as Lieutenant Portas, wears the full dress uniform usually reserved for home service. Note the ribbed lace edging, and long loop over the national cockade, on his cocked hat. His belt plate clearly bears the ornamental letters 'G C' either side of the Royal Arms. His coat is dark blue with red facings on collar and cuffs, while his shoulder and waist belts are of yellow buckskin. During 1898, Lieutenant Portas was accused of committing atrocities against Cuban prisoners incarcerated for involvement in bomb throwing plots. From 'A Photographic History of the Spanish-American War' (1898).

A detachment of the Civil Guard in Cuba. They wear the blue-grey campaign dress with red collar and cuffs, and round, grey felt hats, some of which are looped up on the left in regulation fashion. Each man has his folded *capote*, or caped overcoat, draped over his shoulder with purple-lined side out. They are armed with the Spanish Remington rifle, and carry 40 rounds in the cartridge boxes worn on their belt fronts. From 'A Photographic History of the Spanish-American War' (1898).

edge and front of waist line were trimmed with heavily-patterned gold embroidery. Cuffs were round and also faced with red cloth, with a band of the same gold embroidery sewn just above. Rank insignia was attached below this on the red cuff, and consisted of a system of stars and strips of lace similar to that worn by the army. Epaulettes worn with both full dress and the frock coat were gold with crown and fouled anchor insignia. Trousers were dark blue with welts of the same gold-embroidered lace as found on the coatee. Head dress consisted of a black cocked hat, or *sombrero*

One of the defenders of Puerto Rico, this unidentified Spanish soldier was possibly a member of the 2nd Volunteer Battalion which was raised in the Bayamon area on the north coast of the island. Note his unusual shoulder knots, buglehorn collar insignia, and trouser seam stripe. Phil Katcher Collection.

A cross of merit of the type worn by Spanish naval officers in **1898.** Ben K. Weed Collection.

A cap plate, or collar insignia, worn by a member of a Havana volunteer unit, bearing the coat of arms of the city. Ben K. Weed Collection.

bicornio, trimmed with broad gold lace.

For daily wear, officers donned a double-breasted frock coat and cap with a plate bearing an erect fouled anchor, surrounded by a wreath, with a crown above. The black patent leather visor was embroidered according to rank. During summer, a white service uniform was worn, with dark blue shoulder straps bearing rank insignia.[209]

A petty officer, 1st class, wore a double-breasted jacket for full dress, with rank insignia consisting of two gold chevrons with speciality mark above. A petty officer, 2nd class, wore a short jacket, or *chaquetilla*, with two rows of seven buttons and a single gold chevron.

For winter dress, ratings wore a dark blue jumper with light blue collar edged with three strips of white tape. A black silk neckerchief was worn under the collar. The jumper was tucked into plain trousers of the same colour. The sailor's white-topped round cap was plain and did not bear the ship's name at that time. A white smock and trousers were worn in tropical climates.

Marine Infantry and Artillery

The National Corps of Marine Artillery, or *Cuerpo Nacional de Artilleria de Marina*, was originally established via the Royal Decree of 29 December 1841. In 1848, it was divided in two with the creation of the Royal Corps of Marine Infantry, or *Real Cuerpo de Infanteria de Marina*.[210]

Originally created to serve in a maritime context, the Marine Infantry was assimilated into the Spanish infantry of the line via the Royal Decree of 27 July 1882. The Marine Artillery continued to serve with the Navy. Three regiments of Marine Infantry, composed of two battalions of five companies each, existed by 1898. This force was supplemented by three Reserve Battalions, three Depot Battalions, three Companies of Artificers and one Company of Clerks. Recruiting for these regiments took place in the three maritime districts of Cadiz, Ferrol and Carthagena.[211]

In 1898, both battalions of the 1st Marine Infantry were stationed respectively in the Cuban provinces of Matanzas and Pinar del Rio, while the second battalions of the 2nd and 3rd regiments were located in Holguin Province. Only one company remained in the Philippines by August 1898.[212]

As a result of the Royal Order of 30 April 1886, the full dress for Marine Infantry officers consisted of a deep blue *guerrera*-style jacket with two rows of seven gold buttons and gold lace shoulder cords. The standing collar was decorated with a gold lace loop and gilt button either side. The cuffs were edged with gold lace bars, above which were three short gold trimmed red *sardinetas*. A series of from one to three gilt stars embellished either the cuff or sleeve above, dependent on whether the wearer was a field or company grade officer. Full dress rank was also indicated via a brass gorget bearing a crown over an upright fouled anchor. Headgear consisted of a dark blue cap with black patent leather visor, with from one to three gold lace bands (dependent on rank), gilt cap plate and gold lace chin strap secured either end by a small gilt button. Trousers were deep-blue with broad red seam stripes, and shoes were black.

The Spanish Asiatic Squadron destroyed in Manila Bay was commanded by Admiral Montojo, who is seen here wearing his full dress uniform of dark blue with gold lace edging and red turned-back collar. From Murat Halstead, 'Full Official History of the War with Spain' (1899).

Officers carried straight swords with gilt hilt, gold knot and ivory grip, set in a steel scabbard suspended from a waist belt worn under the jacket, with black leather slings passing through an opening near the left jacket waist seam.

For full dress, Marine Infantry enlisted men wore a deep blue jacket with two rows of seven buttons, shoulder straps of the same cloth edged with red, and solid red wings or pads. Round cuffs were piped with red and embellished with three yellow *sardinetas*. Headgear consisted a *Leopoldina* cap with deep blue body and red band around the top. Worn at the front was a national cockade with red worsted loop, surmounted by a socketed gilt grenade with small red plume.

After 1886, Marine Infantry enlisted men wore a deep blue pullover shirt, or smock, of coarse wool with box pleat fastened by two small gold buttons. The collar was deep blue with gold lace trim and cuffs were plain. Dark blue shoulder straps were piped red and terminated at the shoulder seam with solid red wings. NCOs wore gold lace chevrons edged with red on the

Ramon Aunon y Villalon, Spanish Minister of Marine, was photographed in 1898 wearing his uniform showing the rank of captain in the Spanish Navy. From 'A Photographic History of the Spanish-American War' (1898).

The *Cuadrilleros*, or Rural Guard, was one of many Spanish militia units in the Philippines until to 1898. Note the very unusual chevrons, or *galones*, on the officers' sleeves. From Murat Halstead, 'Full Official History of the War with Spain' (1899).

Opposite.

These two quayside scenes, possibly taken at Manila by the banks of the River Pasig, contain a wealth of information about both the Spanish Navy and Marines. The Marine Infantry unit seen in both photos wears a service uniform, possibly of *rayadillo*, and white barracks caps, whilst the Navy personnel appear in their white tropical kit. Note the naval 'colour party' receiving a salute, and the band in sun helmets in the bottom left of the top photo. Museo del Ejército, Madrid.

lower sleeves. Headgear consisted of a dark blue barracks cap with red band around and black leather chin strap secured by two small gilt buttons. Trousers were dark blue with red seam stripes. An all-white version of this uniform, with barracks cap, and minus trim and facings, was worn in tropical climates.

The Marine Infantry regiments in Cuba during 1898 wore a *rayadillo* campaign uniform with deep blue facings on the collar, cuffs and trousers seams. A metal fouled anchor device was attached to the collar, and three *sardinetas* were sewn on each cuff. Home Marine battalions began to wear this uniform at Cadiz and Cartagena during 1898.

On 5 April 1897, the Marine Infantry detachment in the Philippines received a summer uniform consisting of a seven-button white jacket with deep blue collar trimmed with gold-lace loops and cuffs of the same colour bearing *sardinetas*. NCOs' chevrons were also of yellow lace. Sun helmets covered in white cotton were decorated with the national cockade pinned to the left side of the band.[213]

Belt, straps, cartridge pouches and bayonet scabbard and frog were all of black leather, while the waist belt was fastened by a brass frame buckle. The Reserve Battalion of Marine Infantry at Cadiz in 1898 was described as being 'armed with the Mauser, and trained in the handling of guns'.[214]

Via the Royal Order of 10 February 1869, the Marine Artillery had adopted the same uniform and articles of clothing as the Navy, with the sole difference that officers wore a 'flaming bomb' device on their collars plus a system of cuff stripes, and enlisted men bore two crossed cannon of red cloth on the lower sleeve of their right arm. A Corporal of Cannon, 1st class, wore on both upper arms two inverted red chevrons and a Corporal of Cannon, 2nd class, a single inverted chevron.[215]

Filipino Forces

The Insurgent army of the Philippines was loosely organised on a territorial basis, with units bearing such designations as the 'Bulacan Battalion' or the 'Calumpit Battalion'. On 21 February 1899, the Nationalist government based at Malolos, about 30 miles northwest of Manila, promulgated a decree which established universal conscription of all males between 18 and 35 years of age. Responsibility for putting the system into practice was placed on the town mayors, or *presidentes*, who were permitted to grant exemption based on the payment of money. Nonetheless, there was never a shortage of recruits. The army around Manila in 1898 has been estimated at between 20,000 and 40,000 strong.

Regarding 'uniforms', the Insurgent forces appear to have worn a mixture of loose overshirts, jackets and trousers, made from a variety of cloth including broad-striped *rayado*, plain white, blue, and even checkered, cotton. Straw hats were essential, and most

This group of captured Filipino Insurgents were photographed by A.F. del Montilla. They wear a mixture of cotton or flannel clothing which bears little resemblance to a uniform. At least two appear to have *rayado*, or broad striped, shirts. Their Spanish guards, armed with M1871 Remington 'Rolling Block' rifles, wear the typical *rayadillo* campaign clothing and carry very large cartridge pouches on their waist belts. Museo del Ejército, Madrid.

Top left and right.
Moro weapons (left) spear heads; (right) *bolo, kriss,* **axe.**
Conrad Cairns Collection.

went in bare feet. According to photographic
evidence, some officers may have been distinguished
by jackets with shoulder straps and darker-coloured
trousers bearing broad seam stripes. Later, when the
war went underground, soldiers found it expedient to
wear non-descript clothing in order to change from
'freedom fighter' to *amigo*.

These men were armed with a variety of captured
Spanish, and later American, weapons, including
Remington and Mauser rifles and Krags.
Accoutrements also appear to have been captured.
Firearms were in such short supply that they were
passed on to new recruits after a soldier had completed
his tour of duty.[216] Several small munitions 'factories'
were established on Luzon Island, where empty
cartridge cases were recycled with poor results. One

Emilio Aguinaldo boarding the U.S.S. *Vicksburg* **after his**
capture on 27 March 1901. He wears what appears to be a
Spanish sun helmet, a light cotton drill blouse and trousers,
and leggings. U.S. Signal Corps Photo No. 111-SC-85795,
courtesy of the National Archives.

A Moro group photographed on Mindanao Island. The man with the round shield appears to be wearing a helmet, whilst another stood fourth from the right seems to be wearing body armour. Museo del Ejército, Madrid.

Insurgent unit was composed of *Negritos*, or pygmy Filipinos of the Aeta tribe, who were armed only with bows and arrows and sling shots. During one engagement, U.S. forces described being opposed by a battalion of 'children' whose defence consisted of throwing stones. [217] Those members of the Insurgent army not armed with rifles often carried the dreaded *bolo*, or long-bladed knife, which proved lethal at close range during engagements such as Balangiga and Catubig. Insurgent artillery was very non-descript and consisted of a variety of muzzle-loading brass cannon left over from the earlier days of Spanish colonisation. The few Hotchkiss and Gatling machine guns they captured were considered so precious they were seldom used in case they were re-taken by U.S. troops.

The U.S. soldier met an entirely new type of opponent when he encountered the Moro, or Mohammedan Filipinos, on the island of Mindanao, who practised polygamy and slavery. A religious fanatic, the Moro believed that the more Christians he killed, the longer time he would have in paradise after his death. Adept not only with the *bolo*, he also carried a long, curved knife called the *barong*, which could lop a man's head off as easily as a sharp knife cuts bread. Led by the Sultan, or *Datu*, of Jolo, who resided on the island of the same name just south of Mindanao, the Moro wore a variety of clothing, including

colourful 'war shirts', loose baggy trousers and turbans. Their war leaders traditionally donned iron or copper helmets, and breast and back plates linked by chain mail, reminiscent of 17th century Spanish armour. This was sometimes worn over leather skirts of buffalo hide. Several Moro battle flags survive, both having red fields which feature a shield and *kriss* sword, with a blue canton bearing five stars symbolising the realm of the Sultan of Sulu.

Periodically a Moro worked himself up into a religious frenzy and ran through the undergrowth intent on killing everything in his path. On these occasions, not even a well-aimed .30 calibre round from a Krag rifle could stop such progress. One eyewitness reported seeing a Moro receive 14 wounds in five minutes, three of which penetrated the brain, and yet the man fought on. [218]

Footnotes and Bibliography

The Bibliography in this volume is presented as footnote references.

1　John C. Calhoun to Andrew Jackson, 23 January 1820, in *Correspondence of Andrew Jackson*, edited by John Spencer Bassett (Washington, 1928), Vol. III, p. 12.

2　Milo Milton Quaife, ed., *The Diary of James K. Polk During his Presidency, 1845 to 1849*, 4 vols. (Chicago, 1910), Vol. III, p. 446.

3　Robert E. May, *The Southern Dream of a Caribbean Empire 1854–1861* (Baton Rouge, 1973), p. 11.

4　Basil Rauch, *American Interest in Cuba: 1848–1855* (New York, 1948), p. 111.

5　*Ibid.*, pp. 97–98.

6　Tom Chaffin, "Sons of Washington": Narciso López, Filibustering, and U.S. Nationalism, 1848–1851', *Journal of the Early Republic*, Vol. 15 (Spring, 1995), pp. 94–95, fn. 28.

7　*Keowee Courier* (South Carolina), 7 June 1850, p. 2, cols. 1 & 2.

8　*Charleston Courier* (South Carolina), 3 September 1851, p. 2, col. 4; citing the Savannah *Republican* of 2 September.

9　Chester Stanley Urban, 'New Orleans and the Cuban Question during the Lopez Expeditions of 1849–1851: A Local Study in "Manifest Destiny", *Louisiana Historical Quarterly*, Vol. 22 (1939), p. 1159.

10　*Lancaster Ledger* (South Carolina), 8 September 1852, p. 1, col. 6; citing the *New York Herald*.

11　Ronald Spector, *Admiral of the New Empire: The Life & Career of George Dewey* (Baton Rouge, 1974), p. 4.

12　Murat Halstead, *Full Official History of the War with Spain* (Connecticut, 1899), p. 304.

13　*Ibid.*, p. 374.

14　Terry D. Hooker, *Spanish American War, 1898. The Cuban Land Campaign: Organizational Data* (El Dorado Books, 1997), pp. 76–95.

15　Gregory J.W. Urwin, *The United States Cavalry: An Illustrated History* (Blandford Press, 1983), p. 169.

16　See J. David Truby, 'Captain Zalinski's Dynamite Gun', *Military Images* (September – October, 1979), Vol. I, No. 2, pp. 2–5.

17　Halstead, *op. cit.*, p. 650.

18　*Ibid.*, p. 650.

19　*Ibid.*, p. 651.

20　Theodore Roosevelt, *The Rough Riders* (New York, 1902), p. 130.

21　Richard Harding Davis, *The Cuban & Porto Rican Campaigns* (London, 1899), pp. 205–206.

22　Charles Johnson Post, *The Little War of Private Post* (Boston, 1960), p. 189.

23　Halstead, *op. cit.*, p. 653.

24　Albert A. Nofi, *The Spanish–American War, 1898* (Pennsylvania, 1996), pp. 335–336.

25　Richard E. Welch, Jr., *Response to Imperialism: The United States and the Philippines–American War, 1899–1902* (Chapel Hill, 1979), p. 25.

26　Unidentified insurgent broadside quoted by William T. Sexton, *Soldiers in the Sun* (Harrisburg, Pa., 1939), p. 239.

27　Catbalogan, P.I. 'The letters of Sgt. Ray Hoover, 43rd Infantry', edited by Ron Beifuss, *Military Images*, Vol. IV, No. 4 (January February 1983), p. 9.

28　Graham A. Cosmas, *An Army for Empire* (University of Missouri Press, 1971), pp. 5–7.

29　*Army & Navy Journal* 4 March 1899, Vol. XXXVI, No. 27, p. 622, col. 3. Hereafter cited as *A. & N. J.*, followed by date, volume, and page numbers.

30　Erna Risch, *Quartermaster Support of the Army – A History of the Corps, 1775–1939* (Washington, D.C., 1962), p. 523, fn. 30.

31　Halstead, *op. cit.*, p. 642.

32　Risch, *op. cit.*, p. 523.

33　*Correspondence Relating to the War with Spain – April 15, 1898, to July 30, 1902* (Washington, D.C., 1902), Vol. I, p. 24. Hereafter cited as *Correspondence*, followed by volume and page number.

34　*A. & N. J.*, 11 June 1898 (Vol. XXXV, No. 41), p. 823, col. 1.

35　Post, *op. cit.*, pp. 8–9.

36　Wiliam F. Stobridge, 'Rendezvouz in San Francisco', *Tennessee Historical Quarterly*, XXXIII (Summer 1974), p. 206.

37　Frederick Funston, *Memories of Two Wars: Cuban and Phillipine Experiences* (New York, 1914), pp. 162–163.

38　Risch, *op. cit.*, p. 503.

39　*Army and Navy Register*, 14 August 1897, cited in Jack D. Foner, *The United States Soldier between Two Wars: Army Life and Reforms, 1865–1898* (New York, 1970), p. 125.

40　Douglas Allen, *Frederic Remington and the Spanish–American War* (New York, 1971), p. 79.

41　*A. & N. J.*, 11 June 1898 (Vol. XXXV, No. 41), p. 811, col. 3; and 18 June 1898 (Vol. XXXV, No. 42), p. 836, col. 1.

42　*Correspondence*, Vol. I, p. 319.

43　*Correspondence*, Vol. II, p. 717.

44　*A. & N. J.*, 27 August 1898 (Vol. XXXV, No. 52), p. 1087, col. 2.

45　Risch, *op. cit.*, p. 524, and fn. 37.

46　Halstead, *op. cit.*, p. 484.

47　*Correspondence*, Vol. II, p. 1024.

48　*Correspondence*, Vol. II, pp. 797, 902 and 1028.

49　See Gilbert A. Sanow II and Michael C. Bruun, 'Uniforms for America's Tropical Empire: The Evolution of the Khaki Coat for U.S. Army Enlisted Men, 1898–1913, Part II', *Military Collector & Historian*, Vol. XXXV, No. 3 (Fall, 1983), pp. 98–103.

50　*A. & N. J.*, 6 May 1899 (Vol. XXXVI, No. 36), p. 840, col. 2.

51　*A. & N. J.*, 3 December 1898 (Vol. XXXVI, No. 14), p. 332, col. 3.

52 P. S. Scarlatta. 'The U.S. M1898 Krag–Jörgensen Rifle', *Classic Arms and Militaria* (June, 1994), Vol. 1, No. 6, p. 24.

53 Halstead, *op. cit.*, p. 645.

54 Scarlatta, *op. cit*, p. 27.

55 *Correspondence*, Vol 1, 114.

56 Post, *op. cit.*, p.199.

57 *Correspondence*, Vol. I, p. 304.

58 *Correspondence*, Vol. I, p. 170.

59 *Correspondence*, Vol. I, p. 350.

60 *A. & N. J.*, 27 August 1898 (Vol. XXXV, No. 52), p. 1090, col. 1.

61 Halstead, op. cit., p. 484.

62 William G. Phillips, 'The Woven Cartridge Belt, 1879–1903, Part II', Military Collector & Historian (Fall, 1992), Vol. XLIV, No. 3, p.111.

63 R. Stephen Dorsey, *American Military Belts and Related Equipments* (Union City, Tennessee, 1984), p. 68.

64 Phillips, *op. cit.*, p. 114.

65 *Correspondence*, Vol. I, p. 350.

66 For a full discussion of canteens see William G. Phillips and Carter Rila, 'Oblate Spheroid Canteens, 1858–1916: a Standard Pattern Recognition Guide', *Military Collector and Historian*, Vol. XLI, No. 2 (Summer, 1989), pp. 66–78.

67 Post, *op. cit.*, pp. 76–77.

68 See J. Phillip Langellier, 'From Blue Kersey to Khaki Drill: The Field Uniform of the U.S. Army, 1898–1901', *Military Collector and Historian*, Vol. XXXIV, No. 4, p. 149, for a discussion of the influence of Theo Bingham and others on this choice of uniform.

69 General Orders No. 38, 7 May 1898, Adjutant General's Office, Washington, D.C. Hereafter cited as G.O. No. 38, 7 May 1898, A.G.O., Washington, D.C.

70 *A. & N. J.*, 21 May 1898 (Vol. XXXV, No. 38), front page; and 18 June 1898 (Vol. XXXV, No. 42), p. 842.

71 G. O., No. 39, 9 May 1898, A.G.O., Washington, D.C.

72 *A. & N. J.*, 21 May 1898 (Vol. XXXV, No. 38), p. 742, col. 3.

73 *A. & N. J.*, 28 May 1898 (Vol. XXXV, No. 39), p. 767, col. 1.

74 *Regulations and Notes for the Uniform of the Army of the United States, 1899*, compiled and edited by Jacques Noel Jacobsen Jr (Staten Island, New York, 1973), n.p.

75 *A. & N. J.*, 4 June 1898 (Vol. XXXV, No. 40), p. 794, col. 2.

76 *Ibid.*, p. 783, front page.

77 *A. & N. J.*, 18 June 1898 (Vol. XXXV, No. 42), p. 842.

78 *A. & N. J.*, 11 June 1898 (Vol. XXXV. No. 41), p. 811, col. 1.

79 G.O. No. 120, 24 October 1884, A.G.O., Washington, D.C.

80 Gordon Chappell, Brass Spikes and Horsehair Plumes: A Study of US Army Dress Helmets, 1872–1903 (Tuscon, 1966), pp. 18–46.

81 *A. & N. J.*, 20 August 1898 (Vol XXXV, No. 51), p. 1055, col. 3.

82 *A. & N. J.*, 29 July 1899 (Vol XXXVI, No. 48), p. 1138, col. 2.

83 *A. & N. J.*, 23 July 1898 (Vol XXXV, No. 47), p. 955, col. 2.

84 Halstead, *op. cit.*, p. 642; *A. & N. J.*, 3 December 1898 (Vol. XXXVI, No. 14), p. 332, col. 3.

85 *A. & N. J.*, 6 May 1899 (Vol. XXXVII, No. 36), p. 840, col. 2.

86 *A. & N. J.*, 30 July 1898 (Vol. XXXV, No. 48), p. 983, col. 3.

87 *A. & N. J.*, 23 September 1899 (Vol. XXXVII, No. 4), p. 37, col. 3.

88 War Department, Office of the Quartermaster General, Spec. 502, 14 February 1900; Spec. 570, 25 March 1902.

89 *A. & N. J.*, 4 June 1898 (Vol. XXXV, No. 40), p. 803.

90 *A. & N. J.*, 23 May 1898 (Vol. XXXV, No. 34), p. 651, col. 2.

91 *Regulations and Decisions Pertaining to the United States Army*, 2nd edition, 20 June 1898, p. 9 (Washington, 1898).

92 *A. & N. J.*, 29 October 1898 (Vol. XXXVI, No. 8), p. 215.

93 *A. & N. J.*, 30 July 1898 (Vol. XXXV, No. 48), p. 983, col. 2.

94 *A. & N. J.*, 13 August 1898 (Vol. XXXV, No. 50), p. 1031, col. 2.

95 *Correspondence*, Vol. II, p. 1028.

96 *A. & N. J.*, 23 September 1899 (Vol. XXXVII, No. 4), p. 79, col. 3.

97 Tom Jones & Fitzhugh McMaster, 'Light Battery G, 6th Artillery, 1899 (Bridgman's Bull Battery)', *Military Collector & Historian*, Vol XXXVII, No. 4 (Winter, 1985), pp. 179.

98 *A. & N. J.*, 23 September 1899 (Vol. XXXVII, No. 4), p. 79, col. 3.

99 *A. & N. J.*, 6 May 1899 (Vol. XXXVI, No. 36), p. 854, col. 1, citing G.O. 80, 24 April 1899.

100 *A. & N. J.*, 4 March 1899 (Vol. XXXVI, No. 27), p. 622.

101 *A. & N. J.*, 4 June 1898 (Vol. XXXV, No. 40), p. 793, col. 2.

102 John Sickles, 'Teddy's Troopers. A look at the Rough Riders of 1898', *Military Images*, Vol. VIII, No. 2 (September October, 1986), p. 8.

103 *San Antonio Express* (Texas), 8 May 1898. Taken from an article entitled the 'Rough Riders Are In Barracks'.

104 John C. Rayburn, 'The Rough Riders in San Antonio, 1898', *Arizona and the West*, Vol. III (Summer, 1961), p. 118.

105 Sidney B. Brinkerhoff, *Metal Uniform Insignia of the Frontier Army, 1846–1902* (Tuscon, 1972), p. 5.

106 Roosevelt, *op. cit.*, p. 54.

107 Virgil Carrington Jones, *Roosevelt's Rough Riders* (New York, 1971), p. 34.

108 Post, *op. cit.*, p. 82.

109 Davis, *op. cit.*, p. 202.

110 *Ibid.*, p. 151.

111 Urwin, *op. cit.*, p. 170.

112 Post, *op. cit.*, p. 83.

113 Citation from Gregory J. W. Urwin, *The United States Infantry: An Illustrated History, 1775–1918* (Blandford Press, 1988), p. 138.

114 John Bigelow, Jr., *Reminiscences of the Santiago Campaign* (New York & London, 1899), p. 98.

115 John H. Parker, *History of the Gatling Gun Detachment, Fifth Army Corps, at Santiago* (Kansas City, Mo., 1898), pp. 178–185.

116 Davis, *op. cit.*, p. 223.

117 Cosmas, *op. cit.*, p. 153.

118 *Ibid.*

119 *A. & N. J.*, 30 April 1898 (Vol. XXXV, No. 35), p. 668, col. 3.

120 *Correspondence*, Vol. I, p. 35.

121 *Correspondence*, Vol. I, p. 42.

122 *Ibid.*

123 *A. & N. J.*, 7 May 1898 (Vol. XXXV, No. 36), p. 763, col. 1; 14 May 1898 (Vol. XXXV, No. 37), p. 715, col. 2.

124 *A. & N. J.*, 30 April 1898 (Vol. XXXV, No. 35), p. 679, col. 2.

125 Charles Johnson Post, 'Collector's Field Book – Memoirs of Cuba, 1898', *Military Collector & Historian*, Vol. V, No. 3, pp. 77–78.

126 Davis, *op cit.*, p. 222.

127 Post, *op. cit.*, pp. 25–26.

128 *A. & N. J.* (Vol. XXXV, No. 30), 26 March 1898, p. 553; citing Fred T. Jane, *All the World's Fighting Ships* (Boston, 1898).

129 *A. & N. J.* (Vol. XXXV, No. 30), 26 March 1898, p. 557.

130 *A. & N. J.* (Vol. XXXV, No. 34), 23 April 1898, p. 653.

131 *A. & N. J.* (Vol. XXXV, No. 42), 18 June 1898, p. 833, col. 1.

132 James C. Tily, *The Uniforms of the United States Navy* (New York, 1964), various pages.

133 *Ibid.*, p. 207.

134 *Ibid.*, pp. 208, 212 and 216.

135 *Ibid.*, pp. 207, 216, 219.

136 Harold L. Peterson, *The American Sword, 1775–1945* (Philadelphia, 1954), pp. 161–62.

137 Michael J. O'Donnell & J. Duncan Campbell, *American Military Belt Plates* (Alexandria, Virginia, 1996), p. 606.

138 *A. & N. J.*, 27 August 1898 (Vol. XXXV, No. 52), p. 1090, col. 1.

139 Harold L. Peterson, *American Knives: The First History and Collectors' Guide* (Highland Park, New Jersey, 1993), p. 103.

140 Robert Debs Heinl, Jr., *Soldiers of the Sea: The United States Marine Corps, 1775–1962* (Annapolis, Maryland, 1962), pp. 111–123.

141 Quartermaster, U.S. Marine Corps, *Regulations for the Uniform and Dress, Equipments, Etc., United States Marine Corps,* Washington: Government Printing Office, 14 July 1892.

142 Edward Scott Meadows, *U.S. Military Holsters and Pistol Cartridge Boxes* (Dallas, Texas, 1987), p. 360.

143 Thomas Arliskas, 'First Marine Battalion, Guantanamo Bay, Cuba June 1898', *Military Collector & Historian*, Vol. XXIX, No. 1, pp. 30–31, 39.

144 Tily, *op. cit.*, p. 238.

145 Grover Flint, *Marching with Gomez* (Boston, New York & London, 1898), p. 116.

146 *Frank Leslie's Popular Monthly* (New York), Vol. XLVII, No. 3 (January, 1899), p. 238; cited in Raymond Johnson & Wayne Colwell, 'Cuban Insurgent Army, 1895–1898', *Military Collector & Historian*, Vol. XLI (Spring, 1989), p. 33.

147 C.T. Cairns, 'Uniforms of Cuba 1868–98', *El Dorado*, Vol. 7, No. 1, p. 26.

148 Flint, *op. cit.*, pp. 55–56.

149 Johnson & Colwell, *op. cit.*, p. 33.

150 Juan Padrón, *El Libro del Mambi* (Havana, 1985), p. 85.

151 Flint, *op. cit.*, p. 36.

152 Padrón, *op. cit.*, colour plate F.

153 Cairns, *op. cit.*, p. 26.

154 *Ibid.*, p. 27.

155 Flint, *op. cit.*, p. 248.

156 *Ibid.*, p. 21.

157 *Ibid.*, p. 29.

158 *Ibid.*, pp. 250–251.

159 Post, *op. cit.*, pp. 131–132.

160 Chaffin, *op. cit.*, p. 98.

161 Cairns, *op. cit.*, p. 27.

162 *A. & N. J.*, 16 April 1898 (Vol. XXXV No. 33), p. 616, col. 1.

163 W. H. Cromie, *The New Organisation of the Spanish Army* (Pallas Armata, 1996; reprint of original article published in the United Services Magazine in 1883), p. 22.

164 *Almanaca de Githa* (1883), British Library Collection, p. 9.

165 Cromie, *op. cit*, pp. 23–24.

166 Allen, *op. cit.*, p. 17. This quote was originally published in the *New York Journal*, 31 January 1897.

167 Leonard Williams, 'The Army of Spain: Its Present Qualities and Modern Virtue', *Journal of the Military Service Institution of the United States*, Vol. XXI, pp. 351–352.

168 Cosmas, *op. cit.*, p. 76.

169 Henry Cabot Lodge, ed. *Selections from Correspondence of Theodore Roosevelt and Henry Cabot Lodge, 1884–1918* (New York & London, 1925), Vol. I, p. 317.

170 Hooker, *op. cit.*, pp. 1–9.

171 Severo Gómez Núñez, *La Guerra Hispano–Americana: Puerto–Rico y Filipinas* (Madrid, 1902), p. 82; Nofi, *op. cit.*, pp. 335–336.

172 *Correspondence*, Vol. II, p. 654; Nuñez, *op. cit.*, pp. 202–203 and 216–217.

173 See *Reglamento de Uniformidad, Aprobado por Real órden de 18 de Agosta de 1886* (Madrid, 1886); Carlos J. Medina Ávila, *Organización y Uniformes de la Artillería Española* (Madrid, 1992), p. 96; J. Albi de la Cuesta & L. Stampa Piñeiro, *Campañas de la Caballeria Española en el Siglio XIX* (Madrid, 1985), Vol. II, pp. 557–558.

174 *Collección Legislativa del Ejército*, pp. 482–484; Servicio Historico Militar. Sección de Ultramar. No copy of 1880 decree has been located.

175 Delfín Salas, *La Guerra de Cuba, 1898* (Aldaba, S.A., 1989), p. 40.

176 My thanks to Jose Manuel Guerrero Acosta for sharing his views on the origins of *rayadillo* uniforms.

177 Flint, *op. cit.*, p. 40.

178 Post, *op. cit.*, p. 192.

179 Roosevelt, *op cit.*, p. 138.

180 See Allen, *op. cit.*, pp. 12 and 81.

181 Luis Fenollosa Emilio, *The Emilio Collection of Military Buttons* (Salem, Massachusetts, 1911), pp. 187–194.

182 Halstead, *op. cit.*, p. 484.

183 Robert W. D. Ball, *Mauser Military Rifles of the World* (Iola, Wisconsin, 1996), pp. 215–220.

184 John Walter, *Rifles of the World: The Definitive Illustrated Guide to the World's Centre–Fire Rifles* (London, 1993), pp. 218 and 220–221.

185 B. Barceló Rubí, *Armamento portabil español 1764–1939* (Madrid, 1976), p. 229.

186 *Reglamento de Uniformidad*, 1886, *op. cit.*, various pages.

187 *Ibid.*

188 Royal Order of 15 November 1879, circular number 152. See also *Reglamento de Uniformidad*, 1886, *op. cit.*, n.p.; *Almanaca de Githa, 1898–1899*, p. 16, British Library.

189 Jose Luis Calvo Peréz & Luis Grávalos Gonzáles, *Banderas de España* (Vitoria, 1983), pp. 190–191.

190 Cairns, *op. cit.*, p. 27.

191 Angel Ruiz Martin, *Evolucion de las Divisas en las armas del Ejército Español* (Madrid, 1982), pp. 63, 65.

192 See 1886 Regulations and José María Bueno, *Soldados de España* (Malaga, 1978), p. 126.

193 West Point Museum Fabricated Exhibit No. 21.

194 Ávila, *op. cit.*, p. 96.

195 Cromie, *op. cit.*, pp. 34–37.

196 Ávila, *op. cit.*, p. 96.

197 Cairns, *op. cit.*, p. 30.

198 J. Albi de la Cuesta & L. Stampa Piñeiro, *Campañas de la Caballeria Española en el Siglio XIX* (Madrid, 1985), Vol. II, pp. 557–558.

199 *Boletín de la Agrupaciónde Miniaturistas Militares*, No. XXI (Barcelona, 1979).

200 Bueno, *Soldados de España*, *op. cit.*, p. 132.

201 *A. & N. J.*, 16 April 1898 (Vol. XXXV, No. 33), p. 616.

202 Cromie, *op. cit.*, pp. 37–38.

203 Emilio, *op. cit.*, pp. 187–88.

204 See Thomas Arliskas, 'The Civil Guard in Cuba 1895–98', *Military Collector & Historian*, Vol. XXVII, No. 2, pp. 76–78.

205 See José Manía Bueno and J. Hefter, 'Cuban Volunteer Battalions 1892–1898', *Military Collector & Historian*, Vol. XVII, No. 2, p. 54.

206 Albi & Stampa, *op. cit.*, Vol. II, p. 559, *Boletin de la Agrupación de Miniaturistas Militares de España*, 3rd Trimester, 1981, pp. 8–9.

207 Bueno, *Soldados de Espana*, *op. cit.*, p. 133.

208 *A. & N. J.* 26 March 1898, (Vol. XXXV, No. 30), p. 553; citing Fred T. Jane, *All the World's Fighting Ships* (Boston, 1898).

209 F. G. Blakeslee, *Uniforms of the World* (New York, 1929), pp. 210–211.

210 José María Bueno, *La Infanteria y la Artilleria de Marina 1537–1931* (Malaga, 1985), p. 8.

211 Cromie, *op. cit.*, pp. 38–39.

212 Hooker, *op. cit.*, pp. 18, 27 and 57; and *Correspondence*, Vol. II, p. 655.

213 Bueno, *op. cit.*, pp. 39–42.

214 *A. & N. J.* 4 June 1898, (Vol. XXXV, No. 40), p. 795, col. 2.

215 Bueno, *op. cit.*, p. 51.

216 F. D. Millett, *The Expedition to the Philippines* (New York, 1899), p. 71.

217 Sexton, *op. cit.*, p. 87.

218 *Ibid.*, p. 234.

Spanish-American War Directory

This directory is a comprehensive guide for Spanish-American War living historians, re-enactors, modellers, and wargamers.

Museums

West Point Museum, situated at the United States Military Academy, West Point, New York 10996, U.S.A., has a collection of uniforms and weapons appertaining to the Spanish-American War period.

The National Infantry Museum, Building 396, Baltzell Avenue, Fort Benning, Georgia 31905–5593, U.S.A., has a considerable amount of material relating to the U.S. Infantry of the period.

Naval Historical Center, 901 M Street SE, Washington Navy Yard, Washington, DC 20374-5060, U.S.A., possesses an interesting collection of Spanish-American War artifacts, including: a chart used by the navigator on USS *Baltimore* during the Battle of Manila Bay; a Hotchkiss rifle captured from the Spanish cruiser *Don Antonio De Ulloa* which fired the last shot at Dewey's fleet; Admiral Dewey's uniform, pennant, sword, and personal effects; and an enlisted sailor's uniform.

The Independence Seaport Museum, 211 South Columbus Blvd & Walnut Street, Philadelphia, PA 19106-3199, U.S.A. (Phone: (215) 925 5439) has care of U.S.S. *Olympia*, the flagship of Commodore George Dewey during the Battle of Manila Bay. Badly in need of repairs, the vessel is at Penn's Landing, adjacent to the Museum. Volunteers and funds are desperately needed to restore her.

Theodore Roosevelt Birthplace National Historic Site, c/o Manhattan Sites, 26 Wall Street, New York, NY 10005 (Phone (212) 825-6880). This site was the home of Theodore Roosevelt for the first 13 years of his life. An extensive museum depicts his life and accomplishments.

Museo de la Revolución, Avenida de los Misiones, La Habana, Cuba (Phone 62–4091) – has a small collection of artifacts and reconstructions relating to the history of Cuba's struggle for independence up to 1898 and beyond.

Museo de la Ciudad, Plaza de Armas, La Habana (Phone 61–0722) housed in the Captain General's colonial palace, contains a very rich display of weapons and artifacts from the wars with Spain including Spanish *rayadillo* uniforms, Cuban and Spanish flags and a Model 1868 75mm Krupp field gun.

Museo del Ejército, Méndez Núñez 1, 28014 Madrid, España (Phone: 91 522 89 77 Fax: 91 531 46 24) has the best collection of artifacts of all periods relating to the Spanish Army. The Colonial Room has an extensive display of weapons, clothing, flags and memorabilia relating to Spain in the Philippines and Cuba. Larger exhibitions contain *rayadillo* and white drill uniforms in the Colonies.

Edificio del Alcázar, Cuesta de Carlos V, nº 2, 45001 Toledo, España (Phone: 925 22 16 73 Fax: 925 21 26 24) also serves as an annex to the Museo del Ejército, and houses an extensive collection of artifacts.

Museo Militar Regional de la Coruña, Plaza Carlos 1, s/n, 15001 La Coruña, España, holds some uniforms and relics associated with Colonial rule.

Collections

The Anne S. K. Brown Military Collection at Brown University has a large number of original drawings and prints, mainly by artists covering the Spanish-American War for the illustrated press. Contact Peter Harrington, Curator, Anne S.K. Brown Military Collection, Box A, Brown University Library, Providence, RI 02912, U.S.A. (Phone: (401) 863 2414, Fax: (401) 863 2093).

Home of 'The Colours' – Militaria and Historical Flag Research – can be found on the Internet (e-mail address: B.K.Weed@Worldnet.att.net). Ben K.

Weed has a large collection of flags and other Spanish-American War related artifacts. Based on nearly 30 years of dealing with countless numbers of flags of many periods, Ben has available to the public exclusive services for old flag identification, dating and re-marketing valuations. He also has many artifacts related to the period for sale. Contact Ben K. Weed, P.O. Box 4643, Stockton, CA 95204-0643, U.S.A.

The Library of Congress holds the Hoes Collection, relating to the Spanish-American War and its results in Cuba, Puerto Rico and the Philippines, which was gathered together by Chaplain Roswell Randall Hoes, United States Navy.

Living History and Re-enactment Groups

'The Spanish-American War, 1898' is a well-established San Francisco Bay Area living history and re-enactment group which may be contacted at: The Spanish-American War 1898, 945 Ponderosa Ave. No. 109, San Jose, CA, 94086, U.S.A.

K Troop, 1st U.S. Volunteers, are a re-enactment group based in Leon County, Texas. Address c/o John Cobb, 8068 PR 1440, Centerville, Texas 75833 (Phone: (903) 536-3332).

The Living History Crew of the *Olympia*, based in Philadelphia, actually live aboard the vessel during weekends when 'on duty'. They perform drills on the 5" and 6 pdr. guns, signalling, single stick drill, small arms drill, and navigation. They have a cook with a functional galley who cooks meals according to the period navy cookbook, and a chaplain who gives church services on the fantail. They have also recreated the USFS *Olympia* Brass Band which specialises in music of the periods. Contact the Independence Seaport Museum, 211 South Columbus Blvd & Walnut Street, Philadelphia, PA 19106-3199, U.S.A. – Phone: (215) 925 5439; or Patrick McSherry, Spanish American War Centennial Website (http://WWW.POWERSCOURT.COM/war/).

Re-enactment Suppliers

F. Burgess & Co., 200 Pine Place, Red Bank, NJ. 07701, U.S.A. (Phone: (908) 576-1624) campaign hats, 1885 cups.

Quartermaster Shop, 5565 Griswold, Kimball, MI 48074, U.S.A. (Phone: (810) 367-6702) '84 & '85 trousers, '83 shirt, '84 blouse, chevrons.

Steve Davis, 7522 W. McKenzie, Phoenix, AZ 85033, U.S.A. (Phone: (602) 849-3737) leggins, haversacks & slings, canteen covers, Krag breech covers.

Frazer Brothers, 5641 Yale Blvd. #125, Dallas, TX 75206, U.S.A. (Phone: (214) 669-1865) 1878 canteen with sling, shirts and trousers (in stock).

C. & D. Jarnigan, PO Box 1860, Corinth, MS 38834, U.S.A. (Phone: (601) 287-4977) ponchos, shelter halves (tent), blankets, miscellaneous tinware.

O'Dea & Co. 3985 Beaver Lane, PO Box 3785, Camp Verde, AZ 86322, U.S.A. (Phone: (520) 567-0007) '83 shirt, '84 blouse, '88 trousers,'84 fatigues.

S. & S. Firearms 74-11 Myrtle Ave., Glendale, NY 11385, U.S.A. (Phone: (718)497-1100) cartridge belt, 'C' clasps (for belt 3ea.) Krag and Trapdoor parts and Stocks.

G. P. C. West Hurley, NY 12491, U.S.A. (Phone: (914) 679-2417) Rifle parts, oilers & tools, Mauser clip-pouches.

Manifest Destiny, 75H Pelican Way, San Rafael, CA 94901, U.S.A. (Phone: (415) 456-1776) surplus ankle boots.

Missouri Boot & Shoe, Route 7, Box 207, Neosho, MO 64850, U.S.A. (Phone: (417) 451-6100) 1892 & 1893 infantry shoes.

Organisations

The South and Central American Military Historians Society produces the bi-monthly journal *El Dorado*, plus *El Dorado Books*, and devotes much of its attention to the study of the Spanish Army in the Americas. Contact: Terry Hooker, 27 Hallgate, Cottingham, North Humberside, HU16 4DN, England (Phone: 01482 847068).

The Company of Military Historians has published many articles on the Spanish-American War period in its quarterly journal, *Military Collector & Historian*. This society has also produced numerous colour plates on the subject in its series 'Military Uniforms in America'. For details on membership write to The Company of Military Historians, North Main Street, Connecticut 06498, U.S.A.

On the Internet (http://204.182.127.43/war/) the Spanish-American War Centennial Website has been established to exchange information on the period and includes articles, military and naval data on both the U.S.A. and Spain, plus book reviews and news on centennial events.

Book Suppliers

Articles of War Ltd., 8806 Bronx Avenue, Skokie, IL., 60077-1896, U.S.A. (Phone: (847) 674 7445, Fax:

(847) 674 7449, e-mail: warbooks@aol.com, Web site – www.sonic.net~bstone/articles) has a wide selection of Spanish-American War and Philippines Insurrection titles.

The Military Bookman, 29 East 93rd Street, New York, NY 10128, U.S.A. (Phone: 212 348-1280), specialises in rare and out-of-print books of the period.

Michael Haynes, 46 Farnaby Road, Bromley, Kent BR1 4BJ (Phone: 01814 601672) sells a limited range of Spanish-American War books, both new and second hand.

The following bookshops specialise in Spanish and Latin American books:

Angél Nartí, Libros Reyes, Eduardo Dato 1, 50005 Zaragoza, España.

Libros Latinos, P.O. Box 1103, Redlands, California 92373, U.S.A.

Howard Karno Books, P.O. Box 2100, Valley Center, California 92082, U.S.A.

Model Soldier and Wargame Suppliers

Frei Korps 15, 25 Princetown Road, Bangor, Co. Down, BT20 3TA, Northern Ireland (Phone: 01247 883187) offers a wide range of Spanish-

A Spanish volunteer bicycle platoon wearing blue service dress. Units like the 1st Volunteer Battalion, or *Tiradores de San Juan*, did sterling work during the American bombardment of Puerto Rico in 1898. The young cyclists carried more than 85 messages in the course of the action. A comparable unit existed in Manila called the Bicycle Section of the Spanish Casino. From 'A Photographic History of the Spanish-American War' (1898).

American War 15 mm. wargame figures.

Miniature Militaria of Montana, P.O. Box 1166, Wolf Point, MT 59201, U.S.A. (Phone: 406 6533, Fax: 406 6533510) has books and figures relating to the period.

Index